THE HIGHEST KNOWLEDGE

The Highest Knowledge

Aurelio Arreaza

Blue Dolphin Publishing

1993

For further information address
Blue Dolphin Publishing, Inc.
P.O. Box 1908, Nevada City, CA 95959

ISBN: 0-931892-52-X

Library of Congress Cataloguing-in-Publication Data

Arreaza, Aurelio, 1945–
   The highest knowledge / Aurelio Arreaza.
     p. cm.
   ISBN 0-931892-52-X : $9.95
    1. Religions (Proposed, universal, etc.) 2. Religions—
Relations. 3. Arreaza, Aurelio, 1945–   —Religion.
I. Title.
BL390.A77 1993
291-dc20   92-41893
                                     CIP

Printed in the United States of America by
Blue Dolphin Press, Grass Valley, California

5   4   3   2   1

THE HIGHEST KNOWLEDGE
about OURSELVES *and* LIFE,
HEALTH, WELL-BEING, *and* YOUTH

We all have a great treasure,
A strong, pure energy within;
The soul, God within;
Richest fountain of knowledge, love, well-being,
Constantly guiding us.
Eternal source of the right decision
For every moment and every occasion.

But our bodies are so intoxicated
By negative food and drink,
Our minds so confused
By negative information,
That most of us don't recognize or listen to
That strong and subtle guidance,
Never achieving the best,
But frustration and unhappiness.

Yet, through proper understanding and care
Of body, mind, and soul,
We will develop our limitless potential,
We will always have beauty, health, and youth,
We will tune more and more to our inner guidance,
We will gradually raise our level of consciousness,
To really enjoy a creative, harmonious life,
Feeling higher and higher.

Table of Contents

Dear Friends:

It was a beautiful and cool November morning in South Miami. I was living in a house with a big garden. There were many trees and plants—some big, some small, some bearing fruits, some giving flowers, many varieties of leaves, a beautiful abundance of semitropical vegetation.

On the back of the house there was a room, windows all around, sort of a porch, with an old sofa from where one could observe a good part of the garden and listen to the birds. To me, loving nature as I do, that was my idea of paradise.

That morning, like many others, I was sitting cross-legged on the sofa engaged with my books and pads. Yet on this occasion I was working on a poem that I would give to Adriana on her birthday. From time to time I would observe with enjoyment and patience the enchanting, varied, and refreshingly green manifestation of life around me.

But soon I recognized that voice again—that already familiar voice that, though coming from within, from my heart, my stomach, also came from faraway, from some infinite point. That voice had firmly directed the most important actions of my life.

This was the basic message: "You can write a book about the highest purpose of life. You have been learning about this subject and practicing related activities for many years. You are ready to understand and write all that I have to tell you. . . . Mankind should have a better knowledge about itself, about its real purpose. It is becoming more and more important. Human beings have a great potential to experience well-being and happiness, but most of them don't live up to it, don't even know about it. . . . Yes, you must share all you know and all that I am going to tell you."

I had been listening to a similar message on and off for the last few days. Now it was clearer and stronger. I felt that I had no choice but to get ready to obey the order. Perhaps the next day. Would I be capable?

I continued working on the poem, then read aloud a good part of an article in *National Geographic*. Around noon I started to get ready to go out, my head full of thoughts about the new endeavor.

But I did not wait until the next day. For years I had the habit of doing some writing or studying for one to two hours before dinner. I could continue doing this in Miami—my roommate had late dinner hours so, fortunately, I was left alone most early evenings.

That very same evening I sat again cross-legged on the sofa, pad and pencil in hand. Then, as I had learned to do long ago, I gently opened myself to whatever "that voice" had to say. As usual, I did not have to wait too long.

"To begin with we must set up the basic plan for the book. It will be easier to work it out from there. It will convey the most important knowledge any one can learn, but in a simple way, so that many people will be able to understand it and relate to it. . . . Though there has been so much true teaching over the centuries, most people are confused or ignorant about the true purpose of life. . . . Of course, there must be one chapter dedicated to the body, another to the mind, and another to the soul. But first an introduction—people should know why this book is being written. . . . Then, maybe another chapter. We'll see when we get there."

The plan felt sensible, and I had total confidence in "that voice"; it had never been wrong. Yet I would have to be very careful and patient. I wanted to convey everything very clearly, and "that voice" was never in a hurry.

But soon I started to think about all the work and time that writing this book might require. Maybe years. . . . How would I support myself? What about getting it published? It did not seem that easy.

"The voice" answered promptly: "You know better than that. No doubt should trouble you. It is a most beautiful and special mission. Everything will be taken care of. . . . The book will convey the most important knowledge—the basic knowledge that really concerns everyone. It will be very clear. . . . Many people will be interested. Many people will read it. Many people will like it. . . . Everything will be taken care of. You know how it is. No doubt should trouble you."

Thus, what you are about to read is the result of many months listening to the subtle communication that came from beyond and within, and several years, also with the help of "the voice," of improving, editing, and reorganizing all that had been written before.

I dedicate this work to you, to all the men and women who by their example, friendship, or legacy have helped me along the way, and to the United States of America whose unique atmosphere of freedom and positivism made it possible.

Sincerely,
Aurelio Arreaza

We are Heirs

to the Limitless Richness

of the Spirit

Introduction

"HUMAN BEINGS ARE, PERHAPS, the most marvelous creatures in the universe—where everything is absolutely related and where a Supreme Intelligence coordinates and maintains all of creation in constant harmonious evolution.

"This coordination and evolution happens through a direct and permanent contact which all living things have with that Supreme Intelligence. This contact is made possible through what can be called 'the all pervading energy'—a divine, strong, and subtle energy that is everywhere, within all beings and things, coordinating life and evolution.

"Most living creatures are contented and at peace, existing and evolving in a natural, harmonious way, just part of the universal evolution or flow. Through this 'all pervading energy,' they simply follow the guidance of God Supreme Universal Intelligence, thus realizing the highest purpose of life.

"Yet human beings, in order to come closer to God's will through a higher dimension, have been given a marvelous capacity for awareness and intelligence, which permits them to analyze and alter their environment, but which can also turn against them. Hence, this capacity has, too often, made them commit the error of going astray from God's guidance and ignoring the will of their Creator, thus being negative to themselves and creating disharmony and negativity around them.

"Each one of us has a different level of consciousness. Depending upon this level, we create different degrees of harmony or disharmony in our environment.

"This level of consciousness is sort of an inner, natural knowledge that dictates the way we relate to everyday life and the world around us. The higher our level of consciousness, the closer we are to the will of our Creator, and the more we will experience awareness, creativity, happiness, and well-being.

"Yet we can use our awareness and intelligence to help raise our level of consciousness or rediscover our direct contact with the Creator. This contact was never broken, only ignored or lost in confusion.

"God Supreme Universal Intelligence, loving and wise, gives us the chance to raise our level of consciousness so that we can improve the quality of our lives. For this purpose we are offered ways to get in closer contact with our soul or 'energy within.' The gradual increase of this contact causes a gradual increase in our level of consciousness, a constant overall improvement of our lives, and a real understanding of the world around us.

"Moreover, this is the only way to achieve individual happiness and well-being and to reach the highest purpose of life: to be our real selves and to live according to our own natural inner guidance, God's guidance. This is also the only way to prevent us from further destruction, misery, and chaos on earth.

"Human beings are composed of body, mind, and soul—three different things closely interrelated and, in certain ways, dependent upon each other. In order to reach higher levels of consciousness and harmony, we should have a clear understanding of our bodies and minds, and work to improve each one of them so that, more and more, they function according to our souls, positively reinforcing one another. This is the only way to constantly reach higher levels of consciousness and gradually improve our life in every sense.

"Therefore, the following pages will present, in a clear and simple way, what our bodies, minds, and souls are and how to take proper care of them.

"We will become more open to this knowledge if it is supported by quotations after every chapter from some of the most enlightened men that have ever lived. These men, with whom many of us are familiar, were also teaching the understanding and care of the body, the mind, and the soul because they knew this was the only way to reach real freedom, happiness, and well-being.

"Thus, to start with, it would be good to offer a brief history about the lives and teachings of these men who, by so closely following the guidance of their souls, became such high and brilliant instruments of God."

*

The voice stopped. I realized this was the introduction. I liked it very much. As I worked to improve it, I felt better and better. It had taken more than two hours of writing and rewriting. I realized that working on this book was going to be an exciting and interesting task.

I felt hungry. It was dark outside. Robert hadn't come home nor called. All I could hear were the sounds from the garden and maybe a cricket or two. I got up, turned on the radio to classical music and went to the kitchen.

Then it came to my mind that if we really want to better understand and digest all that is going to be written in this book, we should read it slowly and aloud. This is what I have been doing for years with almost everything I read, and it really works. Maybe I read less, but what I read I certainly understand and make mine.

All men are born to reach perfection.
Each one will reach it by performing his natural duty.

Krishna, Bhagavad-Gita

God is all that a man may desire
Without transgressing the law of his nature.

Krishna, Bhagavad-Gita

There shall be one standard for you;
It shall be for the stranger as well as the native.

Moses, Leviticus 24

For six days work may be done,
But on the seventh there is a sabbath of complete rest;
Holy to the Lord;
Which must be dedicated to Him.

Moses, Exodus 31

There is a state of bliss
In which we can perceive the real value
Of all that previously formed the constant of our lives.

Buddha, Doctrine of the Buddha

Truth is above sectarian dogmatism.
Only in Truth there is salvation.

Buddha, Doctrine of the Buddha

Seek not the Law in your scriptures,
For the Law is life, whereas the scripture is dead.
I tell you truly,
Moses received not his laws from God in writing,
But through the living word of living God
To living prophets for living men.
In everything that is life is the Law written.
You find it in the grass, in the tree,
In the river, in the mountain,
In the birds of heaven, in the fishes of the sea;
But seek it mainly in yourselves.
For I tell you truly,
All living things are nearer to God
Than the scripture which is without life.
God so made life and all living things
That they might be the ever-living word that
Teach the laws of the true God to man.
God wrote not the laws in the pages of books,
But in your heart and in your soul.
They are in your breath, your blood, your bone;
In your flesh, your bowels, your eyes, your ears,
And in every little part of your body.
They are present in the air,
In the water, in the earth, in the plants,
In the sunbeams, in the depths and in the heights.
They all speak to you
That you may understand the tongue
And the will of the living God.
But you shut your eyes that you may not see
And you shut your ears that you may not hear.
I tell you truly
That the scripture is the work of man,
But life and all its hosts
Are the work of God.

Jesus, *Essene Gospel of Peace*

Allah created the heavens and the earth
To reveal the Truth
And to reward each soul according to its deeds.
None shall be wronged.

Mohammed, *Koran* 45

He raised the heavens on high
And set the balance of all things,
That you might not transgress it.
Give just weight and full measure.

Mohammed, *Koran* 55

The Great Masters

Again it was a beautiful morning. As I entered the back room with the big windows, I saw the hummingbird doing its early round on the flowers. I felt good—as usual I had taken my shower and done my morning practice: some prayer, a few Yoga postures, a little workout, and some meditation. I was ready for "the voice" and looking forward to the session—I have always been eager to learn. I sat in silence waiting for "it" to manifest.

*

"THE MORE WE LEARN ABOUT THE FASCINATING LIVES of the unique men who, by the will of God, dedicated themselves to teaching others how to really improve their lives, the more we will understand and realize that they were basically teaching the same knowledge and that their knowledge is definitely related.

"In other words, Krishna, Moses, Buddha, Jesus and Mohammed, from whose lives and teachings the great religions of today originated, were simply teaching their fellow men how to get closer to God's will and harmony in order to feel better and better, how to live trying to fulfill the highest purpose of life.

"KRISHNA. 2000 B.C.? Hinduism, a beautiful and practical religion, was developed from the knowledge and teachings of Krishna, an exceptional man who, following many years of discipleship and learning, was initiated in the essence of the ancient knowledge of the Vedas.

"The Vedas, the oldest known writings about life's basic knowledge, were probably completed by the disciples of the legendary, great master Rama. He was an outstanding man and great teacher who, thousands of years ago, rejecting primitive polytheistic tribal religions, migrated from primeval Europe with hundreds of followers to the area around the upper Indus river. There they started a new way of life under the monotheistic concept, following the guidance of God.

"Legend says that in his youth, Rama, being unable to accept the primitive cults of his native region, travelled to the warmer, southern lands where he had heard that great civilizations existed based upon different religious concepts.

"There he remained for a long time, living in the temples as a devoted disciple and learning all he could. Finally, the most sacred practices, which only a few ever learned, were revealed to him. This was the essential knowledge of ancient masters who already believed in one God and from whose extraordinary and effective teachings the first great Middle Eastern civilizations evolved.

"He remained among his teachers until he thoroughly understood and mastered their disciplines. Later, feeling sure of his knowledge and destiny, Rama returned to the green forests of his native lands up north where he started teaching the Truth. However, this brought him into conflict with other people as he was unable to convince the majority. Therefore, he decided to migrate with many followers in search of a new homeland in a region with a milder climate. This was the historic and significant migration of the Aryans to the area around the upper Indus River. In the new land, satisfying both their material and spiritual needs, the new community began to live and flourish under the natural laws of God.

"Centuries later, Krishna, another very special product of mankind's evolution on earth, after many years of learning and practicing the teachings handed down from Rama, decided to clarify, organize, and revivify that important knowledge.

"The result was Yoga, a number of activities designed to bring a man in ever closer contact with his soul in order to reach higher levels of consciousness and ultimately 'union with God.' This practical knowledge was so effective and enjoyable that it became the essence of Hinduism, the oldest among today's great religions.

"Yet, not much later, organized religion in India started to develop, and some of its leaders, presumably to protect their high status and ascendancy over the population and trying to create a stable social order, established a stagnant, ungodly, and unnatural caste system, affirming that along with the teachings of Krishna it also was God's will. This artificial way of strictly dividing the population into different social classes was to bring endless misery, tragedy, and religious deterioration to that nation.

"Many centuries later the caste system was officially eliminated by the Indian Parliament shortly after that country gained its independence from the British, but only in theory. No doubt Krishna, being a real man of God and absolute believer in the natural laws of the universe, would never have devised a system that would bring artificial division between human beings, much less such an absurd, cruel, and unfair one as the caste system turned out to be.

"Finally, as a result of all this conceptualizing and organizing of a religion by mediocre men, the beautiful, effective, and practical method taught by Krishna was mostly lost and forgotten."

*

I waited and nothing else came out. This seemed to be enough about Hinduism. I began to understand the evolution of religions a little better. Very interesting indeed, exciting.

I saw Bucky, our white poodle, down on the floor, eyes open, his head resting between his legs in his "being bored" position. I decided to stop for a while and take him out to the garden.

Then I felt like eating something. Can I call it breakfast? For years I have had the habit of having my first meal past mid-morning after most of my writing. When my body and energy are not engaged in digestion, writing comes out much better.

So that day I made my usual bowl of rolled oats with some raisins, nuts, seeds, and a sliced banana—all soaked in water, well mixed, and uncooked.

This simple breakfast makes me feel great, full of energy, my brain clear and fresh. It is one of the good things that through the years has been revealed to me.

I sat to eat it, looking at the beautiful vegetation around me, just waiting to go out to enjoy it more.

But it was still early. I decided to keep on writing for a while.

*

"MOSES. 1300 B.C. Now, following a chronological order, we come to Moses—a magnificent, spectacular man who through the ages has inspired much admiration and awe for his amazing feats. He also forms part of the God-designed chain of great men whose destiny has been to reach enlightenment—thanks to their own inspiration and the knowledge of others before them—to finally devote their lives selflessly for the benefit of mankind, inflamed by the courage and perseverance that only the Truth brings.

"As many know, a royal princess, sister to Pharaoh, found a strong, healthy baby on the banks of the Nile and decided to raise him as her son. Thus the boy, whose origin was probably Jewish, grew up as a prince with an Egyptian name in the midst of one of the most civilized monarchies that ever existed with all the privileges that such a situation offered.

"From the beginning he felt a special interest in the realm of the spirit and gradually spent more of his time in the seclusion of the sacred temples where he was exposed to the highest knowledge then available. This knowledge must have been very advanced since it supported such a formidable nation.

"In the temples, where only a handful had access, he joined other disciples under the direction of the high priests. There he did all he could to strengthen his body and follow more and more the guidance of his soul in order to become a real man.

"He did so well that he finally became one of the chosen few to attempt the physical and spiritual tests required to receive the highest knowledge—extremely difficult trials during which some aspirants lost their lives or their minds.

"He emerged victorious and the highest knowledge was revealed to him by the high priests. Now he could be on his own.

"After many years of practicing the activities which formed part of this knowledge, he came to understand the essence of life and gradually reached enlightenment—even surpassing his teacher's understanding and knowledge about life—thus becoming much stronger, self-reliant, and clearer about his life and destiny. Finally he was able to make the decision to try to liberate his people, lead them out of Egypt, teach them the Truth, and take them to another land to start a new life—all of which he accomplished in spite of enormous difficulties.

"So good, logical, and strong was his teaching, that it aroused thousands and motivated a religion that still exists today.

"Moses can be considered the first of the Great Masters who openly brought to the world, in a clear way, the notion of one God which until then only a few had the privilege to enjoy.

"If we carefully read the Old Testament, we can easily realize that Moses was teaching practical ways to achieve 'union with God' by way of taking special care of the body and the mind in order to come in closer contact with the guidance and power of the spirit.

"Yes, we could say that, in a sense, the Jewish people were chosen by God—chosen to convey to the world around them the crucial and absolute truth that there is only one God, under whose direction all men can live in creative harmony and peace.

"Unfortunately, they did not understand their mission but instead isolated themselves in their rituals, traditions, and negative pride in being 'God's chosen people.' Then they complicated their lives with innumerable, unnecessary laws that led them away from reality, spontaneity, and real union with God.

"So strong was this attitude that, centuries later when Jesus, one of their own, came out in a beautiful, high, and strong way, talking about one God for all and teaching the Truth, they were unable to listen to him.

"Today, still waiting for the 'Messiah,' still giving too much importance to rituals, tradition, and little laws, the Jewish people still do not understand that anyone on earth who attains Truth becomes a Messiah. Still many of them do not understand that all human beings are equally loved creatures of God."

*

This was a beautiful and interesting story that transported me to another world, a very special period of our history. Suddenly Moses and the Jews had become more alive and accessible to me.

Every time I think about the Jews and their evolution, I try to understand, but have never been able to come to a definite conclusion. I have been puzzled all my life that so much persecution has been directed against them throughout their history. Why would so many diverse people endlessly persecute a special group of others?

Is it because, considering themselves to be "God's chosen people," they regard themselves as superior to the rest of humanity and so have kept closely and selfishly knit, thus provoking antagonism in others?

In any case, all this hostility and persecution is a great tragedy and brings much negativity to all of mankind, especially the Western world. Let's hope that some day it will come to an end.

We are all equally loved creatures of God and have come to this planet just to learn, understand and love ourselves and others, evolve for the better, and enjoy life.

I felt good; it had been a great morning. I really liked what I had written.

*

"BUDDHA. 550 B.C. We cannot help but feel boundless admiration and reverence for the infinitely compassionate man known as Buddha, the 'Illuminated One.'

"The eldest son of a rich, princely family, he was destined to inherit illustrious titles and much wealth and would be expected to do his best to keep up and improve the family's status. Legend says that he was especially shocked the first time he came out of his beautiful family estate and saw so many others living in helpless misery. Thereafter he began to realize that he did not feel really contented and that there must be something else that life had to offer.

"His only choice was to start searching in a realm he had never paid much attention to before: the spiritual dimension. He started with the ancient and current teachings of his family religion, Hinduism, and became the disciple of some of the gurus and teachers around his hometown.

"After years of practicing different kinds of Yoga and gradually reaching higher levels of consciousness, he realized the magnitude of the path that lay before him. Yet he decided to follow his destiny and left wife, children, family, and riches in order to continue to search, learn, and practice, until he could reach that highest state he so eagerly aspired to.

"Many years passed during which he had numerous adventures and experiences, many ups and downs. But his strong will and steadfast faith never failed him, and at last he was rewarded the highest treasure.

"The more he learned, became whole, and raised his level of consciousness, the more he understood and loved mankind, so

much so that he decided to devote his life to teaching the knowledge he believed would bring peace and happiness to others.

"It can be said that he preached a reformed Hinduism since
he disagreed with some of its concepts. Yet so attractive and
precious was the knowledge he taught that soon he had many
disciples and followers who, after his death, developed Buddhism,
one of the most important religions that has ever existed and which
today is still practiced by millions all over the world.

"Buddha established a path to achieve freedom and happiness
that rejected all conceptual and ritualistic forms of Hinduism
which at that time had already degenerated into a source of despair
and misery for much of the population. Yet most of the essence of
Hinduism, such as the practice of different activities to purify the
body and the mind, were preserved.

"He identified the Four Noble Truths: life is suffering; the
cause of suffering is selfish desire; the way to eliminate suffering is
by elimination of selfish desire; the way to eliminate selfish desire
is by practicing the Eightfold Path: right knowledge, right intention, right speech, right behavior, right livelihood, right effort,
right mindfulness and right absorption.

"His teachings, though not quite simple, could ultimately
bring much well being and contentment to those who practiced
them; however, they were preceded by an exaggerated rejection of
Hinduism, by too much coldness and intellectualism, and by an
apparent denial of a Supreme Being. All of this constantly confused his followers, who at his death created a religion based on his
main concepts with all the ceremonies and rituals he so denied and
which has suffered many divisions over the centuries.

"One of Buddha's most important teachings is: 'Be you lamps
unto yourselves. Those who, either now or after I am dead, shall
rely upon themselves only and not look for assistance to anyone
besides themselves, it is they who shall reach the very topmost
heights.' This is, no doubt, a good intellectual concept. But is it
really true?

"Most of us are somehow confused and weak, especially at the beginning of the path, yet have the natural desire to obtain some degree of information from other people who have reached higher levels of consciousness, as well as the desire to share with others some of the activities practiced to reach 'union with God.' "

*

It was time to make dinner. I had an arrangement with Robert to cook dinner twice a week. Tomorrow I would continue.

Learning about Buddha had been interesting. I couldn't wait to hear what the "voice" had to say about Jesus. He had always been such a towering figure to me. Perhaps too much so. The more I learned, the more I realized that the "Highest Teacher" is within us, and we must not overly rely on anybody else.

Yet I was eager to hear about Jesus, whom I considered to be such a unique, fascinating, heroic, and sublime man.

The next morning, though, I decided to devote some time to Adriana's poem. Her birthday would be in a few days, and I wanted it ready for the occasion.

This very special woman and dear friend came from South America. She inherited from her Spanish, German, and Italian ancestors her very white skin and exuberant red hair.

The poem was just description and praise—description and praise of her physical beauty and delightful behavior. I especially enjoyed working on it.

But before I continue my work with the "voice," I want to point out that the following concepts have the same meaning: enlightenment, the highest purpose of life, to attain freedom, to be our real selves, to reach harmony, union with God.

*

"JESUS. This man was so sure of himself and of what he was doing and teaching, that he did not mind risking his life, defending the Truth under unfair trial, and eventually walking to his death with divine and serene composure.

"He was born into a Jewish family at a time when God and religion were very important to his people, who then lived under the rule of Rome which was civilized enough to believe in religious tolerance as long as it did not threaten the empire.

"Sadducees, Pharisees and Essenes were the principal Jewish sects in those days. The latter followed stricter purification rites and tried to anticipate the Kingdom of God on earth. They tried to achieve this by practicing a special care of the body and the mind that they believed would eventually bring them to awareness of God's will in every circumstance. They lived in brotherly love where righteous word and deed were the highest goal.

"Jesus' parents were practicing Essenes who lived a construc-tive, orderly, and simple life, doing their best to be in harmony with God's natural laws.

"In any case, Jesus, of extraordinary intelligence and sensitiv-ity, was raised in a loving positive atmosphere in close contact with all the spiritual knowledge then available, including the teachings of Moses as interpreted by his parents.

"As he grew up and became a man, he did not feel satisfied with that knowledge. He continued his search where anyone with high spiritual aspirations would have gone—the then far away lands where the most important civilizations and religions existed: Egypt, Persia, India, Greece.

"During his time it was easy to travel. The world had political stability, and the roads were safe thanks to the order imposed by the Roman legions. Thus, for many years Jesus travelled and lived in several countries, learning from everyday life, acquiring the highest knowledge in the temples, being in close contact with the men that had achieved the highest levels of consciousness, and enjoying the beautiful adventure of his life. No doubt he gradually felt better and higher and eventually reached enlightenment.

"His goal fully accomplished, he decided to return to his native land and teach all he had learned so that everyone there could know about the real purpose of life and experience happiness and well-being.

"He spoke about his travels and the knowledge he had acquired in foreign lands. Years later, as some of his followers organized a religion under the banner of Christ-God and worked at putting together the New Testament to serve their purposes, they must have decided to remove all narratives concerning his journeys. By deifying Jesus, they believed that their religion would have more ascendancy over the people, and, of course, God would never have gone any place to learn about the spiritual dimension from human teachers.

"Today, after the discovery of several ancient manuscripts, it is well known that even during Jesus' lifetime there was basic disagreement among his followers on this crucial matter.

"There were those who said he was God, and there were those for whom he was just a great teacher of life—an extraordinary man who was teaching others the highest knowledge they could ever learn.

"The first group, being fanatics, talked about love but did not really experience it, much less understand it or convey it. They followed Jesus everywhere, spoke about him all the time, and competed for his attention.

"The second group practiced every day, with discipline and humility, the spiritually oriented activities learned from Jesus, increasingly feeling and enjoying the marvelous results. They led constructive, harmonious lives, following God's guidance, and truly learning to love themselves and others. They became independent of their teacher, just as he had advised, continuing to love him and considering him their spiritual guide.

"Logically, after the master's death there were serious disagreements among his followers, a conflict that endured for centuries.

"The first fanatic faction, declaring all other groups blasphemous heretics, steadily worked at organizing a religion based upon complicated concepts and rituals, under the banner of Christ-God.

"The second group, living with a discipline that evolved naturally, without the fanaticism of the other, did not intend to form a religion. They were contented with their lives and, knowing that God is within every man, did not expect to have a monopoly on God. They were just happy to keep on practicing and spreading, to those who wanted to hear, the wonderful teachings of Jesus.

"Centuries later, for political purposes, the Roman emperor accepted Christianity and made it the official religion of the decaying empire. He gave the first faction complete authority over the new faith.

"Other Christians were persecuted and their writings destroyed until almost nothing was left of them. The new church of Rome, claiming a monopoly on God and backed by the Roman Empire, compromised more of its already confused spirituality. Then it got into a pattern of material gain, political power, and spiritual domination, which to this day has been the cause of many misfortunes to mankind. Yet men like Martin Luther started to denounce the church's abuses and wrongdoing and called for reform. Since then many other Christians have disagreed and protested against the Roman church, and many new branches of Christianity have developed.

"Like many other institutions, the church of Rome has had its positive aspects. There can be no doubt that it is one of the outstanding products of mankind's evolution on earth. Yet the act of deifying Jesus, of making him like God, has had an enormously significant and tragic impact that has caused, to put it mildly, much confusion, injustice, prejudice, and violence to mankind. It is sad to realize that in his name so many deplorable actions have been and still are committed.

"If Jesus lived today he would not support many of the actions, concepts, and dogmas of some of the churches functioning under his name. Instead of brotherhood, freedom, and love, they have contributed to much of the aggressiveness, confusion, and unhappiness that now exists in the world.

"Jesus was just a wonderful human being who never said that he was the Son of God in the sense that most Christian churches profess. Yes, he was the son of God, as all men are, but much more so, for he really dedicated his life to do all he could to follow God's guidance, to truly be 'one with God.' Anyway, to love and worship him, it is not necessary to believe that he was God. On the contrary, it is more beautiful, natural, and positive to relate to him as a man who, by his magnificent example and teachings, demonstrated to others that they also have the potential to make life a divine and wonderful experience."

*

Thank God that he ever lived. Jesus, my friend, thank you so much for doing all you did; thank you for giving me so much.

I remained in silence for a while. Then a beautiful, big, blue bird landed on a branch near me. It stayed there for a few moments, sort of cleaning its beak with a stem, shaking its tail streaked with white. I watched it the whole time, enchanted.

To fly. . . . How wonderful to be able to fly, freely, whenever, wherever. . . . I have had very lively dreams where I have been slowly flying, looking at everything around and under me. Those have been my most enjoyable, fascinating, and memorable dreams.

*

"MOHAMMED. 550 A.D. Mohammed was the last of the well-known Great Masters, and his divine inspiration, the Koran, became the essence of Islam, the last of the great religions. He is another of the few giants produced by mankind's evolution on earth.

"Before Mohammed's time, Arabia consisted of many different tribes, independent from one another and worshipping many gods. They lived in constant turmoil and indulgence in sensual pleasures.

"The cultural and political center was the city of Makkah, where yearly pilgrimages were held to worship the gods in the sacred sanctuary, the Haram.

"Part of their heritage was the ancient monotheistic tradition of the Semitic people for which Abraham was one of the main sources and from whom they claimed to descend. This tradition was reinforced by the Jewish communities living in Arabia which represented a close contact with the teachings of Moses. In addition, there were the recent teachings of Jesus which had remained very pure thanks to early Christian groups who had settled in Arabia trying to avoid contact with the Roman Empire and later with the Roman Church.

"Members of a special group of individuals called the Hanij, who usually belonged to one of the outstanding Arab tribes, refused to worship many gods. Although they professed adherence to the monotheistic faith of Abraham and the early prophets of the Semitic people, the Arabs regarded them highly, and the term Hanij acquired the meaning of moral uprightness and rectitude. They commanded respect and trust wherever they went for they were above tribal solidarities and differences.

"Mohammed's first contact with the world was precisely in the city of Makkah where, orphaned early, he grew up in the household of his grandfather who belonged to one of the most ancient and influential tribes.

"Early in life he benefitted from the beautiful, calm, and inspiring atmosphere of the desert, for he worked as a shepherd, taking care of the family flocks. Then he was exposed to the different religious beliefs and spiritual knowledge of the various communities that surrounded him.

"He was strongly drawn to the spiritual dimension and dedicated more and more time to exploring it through all the means available. He listened to what others had to say and read whatever seemed interesting, but, of all that information, he only accepted what felt right in his own heart. He also started to practice several activities in order to purify his body and his mind and become closer to his soul.

"Mohammed had an impeccable character. His contemporaries knew him to be an example of honesty and truthfulness. Anecdotes from early periods of his life tell about his intuitive brilliance, profound wisdom, and the determination to learn about the true purpose of a man's life and his relationship with God. He was often lost in deep thought and felt the need to regularly withdraw to a cave as a solitary retreat.

"Eventually he married a rich and supportive widow, had six children, and, working as a merchant, enjoyed a happy family life for several years. Yet he continued to achieve, through the constant practice of various activities, higher levels of consciousness and harmony.

"Legend says that about mid-life he began to have visions and hear voices telling him to dedicate himself to the service of God. Finally, feeling sure of his divine mission, he started to teach what he believed, gaining many followers over the years but having to contend with strong opposition. To achieve his goal, he organized his followers, and, through persuasion and military conflict, he finally succeeded in establishing his one-God religion in Arabia. He became a great political and religious leader whose influence is still one of the strongest in the world.

"Mohammed considered himself the true exponent of the teachings of Moses and Jesus—the one who had rightfully understood them and was properly conveying their message. He believed the essence of that message had been blurred and confused by fanatics, mixed-up writers, and centuries of erroneous interpretation and translations.

"Over a period of twenty-three years, he wrote the *Koran*, a book about the wisdom of life that established the tenets of the new religion. Yet he considered himself as only a channel of the word of God and the *Koran* as the only miracle that God worked through him. Therefore, Moslems consider the *Koran* and not Mohammed as the cornerstone of their faith.

"He often stressed the purely human nature of Jesus, saying, 'Praise me not as Jesus is erroneously praised. For, like him, I am only a man whose destiny is to understand and communicate the will of God.' Thus, the fundamental formula and first pillar of the Moslem creed became: 'There is no God but Allah, and Mohammed is his prophet.'

"Prayer, the second pillar of Islam, is highly regarded by the *Koran* which recommends its practice at least five times a day.

"The third pillar is Charity, another well-known activity among all religions.

"The fourth pillar is the observance of Ramadan, the holy month in the Arabian calendar, during which, among other religious practices, fasting and moderation in drink and food are strictly observed.

"The fifth and last pillar of Islam is a pilgrimage to Mecca, which every Moslem should do at least once in his lifetime.

"The new religion, instead of being called 'Mohammedanism,' was called Islam, which fully translated means 'the perfect peace that comes when one's life is surrendered to God.' After Mohammed's death and over the centuries, Islam also suffered a few divisions, though much less than most other faiths. Yet it must be acknowledged that it is a religion which very much succeeds in having its followers practice its main tenets."

*

I was pleased to learn "the voice's" message about Mohammed and Islam—it is part of the spiritual development of mankind about which I knew little and which very much interested me. I have always wanted to better understand the Arab world and its evolution—it is such an important part of humanity.

Although some of us may not agree with everything Mohammed did or said—for he even raised armies to impose his beliefs, and his followers have been some of the most fanatical people yet known—we must acknowledge that the essence of his doctrine and its practice must produce a deep spiritual satisfaction, otherwise it would not be so fervently observed by so many millions around the world.

Yet some religions tend to overly interfere with the life of their followers, even to the point of cruelty. We must bear in mind that the conditions of the world and the general education of humanity by the time these religions came to be, were very different from the present, and some of their laws and rituals seem too much for these times.

If one practices any activity or doctrine compelled by fear or force, one does not gather the highest results. Most human beings have always needed to practice some kind of spiritual activities in order to feel better; most have always been looking for something to practice, especially when their hearts can follow it with freedom and no pressure. Only such practice can bring the best results.

It is necessary to point out that the religion of Islam tends to impose a theocratic system which means that the government of the country must follow its religious principles and laws. This political-religious approach to government deprives the population of the spiritual liberty essential to each man's successful existence and, as a result, to the successful existence of the whole country.

Each human being should be free to have the kind of spiritual relationship with God that he or she really feels. In a truly harmonious nation there cannot be any kind of religious imposition or discrimination. Church and state must be two separate things. Yet the citizens of a country, for their own sake, should protect and respect, through their government, all religious groups. Otherwise it is impossible to live with dignity and harmony, and achieve true well-being and prosperity.

I felt tired, I had been writing all morning. But I felt good. I sensed I was writing something really important. I just needed to eat something, get my bike, and head towards the park.

I spent most of the afternoon in the park near the ocean. I really liked to go there. To sit on the grass under the coconut trees looking at the wonderful lively ocean, at the suggestive ever-changing clouds, the swift sail boats, the graceful, innocent birds. To slowly read aloud my books and magazines. To walk around and observe the people. To do a good session of Hatha Yoga facing the descending sun. And, if the water was not too cold, to swim for a while in the big, circular, salt water pool.

That park, where I went almost every day, was a corner of paradise that I had found for myself. The time spent there certainly helped to renew the strength of my body, the peace of my mind, and the connection with my soul.

Later that evening, I was more than ready to continue my work. I felt "the voice" more than eager to continue delivering its message.

*

"IN CONCLUSION, IT IS NOT NECESSARY to become an expert on the lives and teachings of the men that most successfully taught others how to get closer to God in order to realize that, somehow, they were all linked to one another and that their knowledge came from the same source: inner revelation and the knowledge of others before them. Moreover, human nature being essentially the same, it is only natural that the basic spiritual needs and religious practices have evolved with so much similarity all over the world.

"It must be understood that in the days of the first great civilizations in Mesopotamia, Egypt, and India, the essential knowledge of how to get closer to God's guidance was only revealed to a few. Most people were more or less satisfied with religious principles, some practices, and rituals to the many gods and goddesses that represented the most important aspects of nature and human qualities.

"As time went by, the great spiritual teachers became less strict about revealing their knowledge. Surely mankind's evolution called for it. Buddha, for example, taught his knowledge to those who proved worthy. Some of his disciples showed their sincere desire to be initiated into this knowledge through years of service, learning, and practice. Some went on to teach their master's knowledge after his death. However, to teach this knowledge properly, a man has to be 'very high,' very close to God's harmony, and even the best disciples did not always reach such a state.

"With Jesus it became easier to learn this high knowledge of life. It was enough to be around him for a few months and, in some cases, even weeks.

"Thus, the knowledge to be conveyed in the following pages is basically the same as what has been taught by the great spiritual teachers since they started their mission thousands of years ago. However, each of them gave more importance to some aspects of the practices than to others, each according to his own experience and feelings.

"This is the knowledge of how to achieve freedom, happiness, and well-being as we get closer to harmony or God's will by means of taking proper care of our body and our mind. This is the highest knowledge about ourselves and life—the knowledge about how to reach the highest purpose of life, the highest freedom, the knowledge about how to become our real, beautiful, loving selves.

"This knowledge will be expressed in the simplest possible manner in the hope that many more of us will better understand ourselves and our relationship to the world, in the hope that it will provide a clear and practical way to increase the enjoyment and quality of our lives."

*

I breathed fully and felt deeply moved. I liked very much what was coming out and felt amazed at how I was writing about the things I was more or less familiar with, as well as many other things I did not know about or about which I had only vague ideas. I was very impressed.

This session had been short, but, the chapter being finished, I decided to wait until the next day to continue.

I looked around the dimly lit house—it felt lonely. Robert and I had been sharing it for a few months. I wished there was a woman with us—a beautiful woman to give it her touch, her liveliness, the magic of her presence.

He fills the whole universe.
He dwells within my heart.

>   Krishna, *Bhagavad-Gita*

You are therefore
To keep all my statutes and all my ordinances,
So that the land
To which I am bringing you to live
Will not spew you out.

>   Moses, *Leviticus* 20

Nirvana is a state
Produced by the destruction of the self,
Marked by a sense of liberation,
Inward peace and strength,
Insight in Truth,
Complete oneness with reality, and
Love towards all creatures of the universe.

>   Buddha, *Doctrine of the Buddha*

Look at this world,
Glittering like a royal chariot.
Only the foolish are immersed in it.

>   Buddha, *Doctrine of the Buddha*

He who conquers himself
Is the greatest of conquerors.

>   Buddha, *Doctrine of the Buddha*

Truth has always been,
For Truth is one and it is everywhere.

>   Jesus, *Aquarian Gospel*

If you bring forth what is within you,
What you bring forth will save you,
If you do not bring forth what is within you,
What you do not bring forth will destroy you.

Jesus, *Gnostic Gospels*

Ask, and it shall be given to you,
Seek, and you shall find,
Knock, and it shall be opened.

Jesus, *Matthew* 7

Yet, the sects are divided concerning Jesus.

Mohammed, *Koran* 19

Tell also of Moses,
Who was an apostle, a prophet
And a righteous man.

Mohammed, *Koran* 19

Allah is One, the Eternal God.
He begot none,
Nor was He begotten.
None is equal to Him.

Mohammed, *Koran* 112

The Body

To Adriana

I

What else can I feel
When your image appears,
Rare open delicate flower,
Orange white tropical fawn.

What else can I feel
When your figure appears,
Dwelling there about my mind,
floating there, sweet, serene.

What else can I feel . . .
But . . . let's be simple,
Why get lost in complicated thoughts
Trying to write precise perfection.

For the more I feel and think,
Attempting to thread the proper sentence,
The more your image brings me pleasure,
Distracting my attention.

I'm surprised to realize
How I can sit such a long time
Enjoying being with you in my mind.

II

No, not with you,
Rare colored exquisite flower.
Let's not use to describe you
Transient common soft adjectives,
As many have done before
With those creatures whom they loved.

No need to mention your heart,
Warm tender boundless wise,
Making of you star bright.
Anybody can feel that.

No need to mention, dear one,
How truth always comes from you;
As in all these months of being,
Here and there, sometimes together,
I have learned without a doubt
That you are someone we can trust.
All your friends for sure know that.

No need to mention your sweetness.
Tender dear delightful sweetness;
Or your willingness to give
Whatsoever one may need;
So much so that usually
Rightly you guess what others want,
Days or moments beforehand,
Giving then so naturally.

Yes, I surely can, for a long time,
Be just with you in my mind.

III

Divine flower, precious treasure,
That sometimes I have the fortune
To be close to and look at,
Rejoicing my heart with that.

It's useless that I keep trying,
As loving bird builds a nest,
To create outstanding poem
describing so much perfection;

Fragile, constant, pure delicacy
Magic colors, sweetest perfumes,
Silken soft, exotic textures.

Much easier would be to fly
Without wings at my own leisure.
So, the only thing left to say:
Being with you is divine pleasure.

*

I looked around me. Still another beautiful day. So many of them in Florida. It can get boring.

It was later than usual. I had gone to bed late and got up late. I did not feel my best. The night before I had too much to eat. I had been to Adriana's birthday party and read the finished poem. Maybe it's a bit long, but they liked it.

I feel great affection for her. She is so sensitive, open, generous, true. . . . She really helped me when I first arrived in Miami. I felt like writing something to express my feelings and gratitude. She can be so sweet. I thought about her and felt good.

I crossed my legs into Lotus position, grabbed the board, pad and pencil, breathed deeply, and waited for "the voice's" word.

*

"THE HUMAN BODY IS A MARVELOUS MACHINE consisting of millions of cells that make up its different parts: bones, inner organs, nervous system, muscles, sense organs, skin, etc. Each one of these cells is an individual living entity that grows, performs its duty, reproduces, and eventually dies. But to do all this successfully, each cell needs a daily amount of proper nourishment—that is, oxygen and nutrients such as carbohydrates, fats, minerals, proteins, and vitamins, that come from natural unprocessed foods.

"Without proper nourishment the cells start to decay, to perform and reproduce unsatisfactorily, to weaken and deteriorate, to finally become victims of disease or infection.

"Some of this illness or deterioration of the cells can be properly detected and present no major problem. But others can go unnoticed, sometimes for years, until the moment when it may be too late to cure them. Especially the so-called degenerative diseases such as arteriosclerosis, arthritis, cancer, diabetes. These are called degenerative diseases because a cell, or a group of weak cells, fall to infection, start to decay and degenerate and to spread their negativity to other cells around them.

"The sad truth these days is that many people do not practice proper breathing nor have a diet which provides all the nutrients they need. In addition to not giving their cells proper nourishment, they attack and poison them with various kinds of toxic substances which only speeds up the process of degeneration and decay.

"Hence, we should be definitely aware that what we take in through our nose and mouth is of extreme importance. Our bodily health and well-being mainly depends on that, which in turn influences our mental health and spiritual development.

"The healthier and stronger our cells, the better our body feels and performs. The healthier and purer our bodies, the higher our awareness and the better we will perform any spiritually-oriented activities to heighten our level of consciousness, creativity, feeling, harmony, and well-being. All this will logically result in a continuous improvement of our body and mind.

"Therefore, if we want our body to perform well and effectively support us in the process of becoming real human beings and fully enjoying life, it is essential that we provide it with the proper daily nutrition and avoid toxins as much as possible.

"It is very important that we develop a balanced and healthy pattern of breathing, drinking, and eating. The quality and quantity of what we breathe, drink, and eat has an immediate and long term effect on how good or bad we feel, how well our body functions, how clear or dull our thinking process is, and how clearly we feel our soul and follow its guidance.

"It is so important to learn to breathe, drink, and eat properly that we must research and study the subject until we feel certain we have found the right information.

"Since many people in their ignorance believe that they already know how to do these things properly, this advice will not seem that important to them—that is, until the time comes when they find themselves feeling sick, spending a fortune on doctors and hospitals that in most cases can do very little for them, and probably learning too late that they have an incurable disease.

"We must realize that being sick is not our natural state, that it need not be part of aging. Being sick is simply the result of not taking proper care of the body, the mind, and the spirit.

"1. *Proper Breathing*. It is surprising that the most vital of the bodily functions is not given more importance in our society nor taught at schools with much more emphasis, for our general health and well-being primarily depends on it.

"When proper breathing occurs, our respiratory system receives a sufficient amount of oxygen that is sent to all the cells of our body by way of our circulatory system. To effectively perform their different functions, the cells need to assimilate nutrients that they receive from the digestive system also by way of the circulatory system. And to properly assimilate these nutrients, the cells need the right amount of oxygen.

"In other words, the food we eat is processed by the digestive system; the resulting nutrients are sent by way of the circulatory system to all the cells of our body where they are assimilated as they come in contact with the oxygen found there.

"Hence, when the cells are given the right amount of energy elements in the form of oxygen and nutrients, they will effectively perform their functions and be much stronger in defending themselves against any form of infection or disease.

"Therefore, proper breathing is the most important activity we can do to keep our bodies healthy and well.

"Moreover, when we don't breathe properly, our whole bodily system feels unsatisfied, causing the nervous system to constantly send a signal to point this out. It is this subtle signal which causes a great part of the nervousness and stress we usually feel.

Yet, in spite of the extreme importance of proper breathing, there are very few people fully aware of this fact, very few breathing properly.

"We experience proper breathing when we inhale and exhale only through our nose, especially when we carefully inhale deeply and exhale completely. It's only when we inhale deeply through the nose that we obtain the proper amount of oxygen that our body needs, and only when we naturally take the time to exhale completely through the nose that we are allowing our body to get rid of the carbon dioxide and stale air that result from the process, making room for a new and proper inhalation.

"Yes, when we carefully inhale deeply and carefully exhale completely, we are giving our respiratory system the proper amount of time that it naturally needs to effectively perform its functions.

"When we unnaturally perform the breathing process through our mouth, we are neither inhaling enough air nor giving our respiratory system the time it needs to function properly. Only in extreme circumstances should we use our mouth for a fast, energy-producing, breathing process. It is good to acquire the habit of keeping our mouth closed unless we are using it for eating or talking.

"Another advantage of proper, natural breathing is that along the inner walls of the nose are specialized hairs that filter many of the impurities from the incoming air."

*

Breathing properly. . . . I had never thought about it like this. It is certainly much more important than I ever realized.

That morning I did not feel like working. I did not feel good. As I said, besides going to bed late, I had eaten too much the night before. All I wanted was to go to the park and relax. I decided to skip brunch and just make myself a nutritional shake.

As usual the park made me feel better. I swam a few lengths across the salt water pool which was about sixty to seventy yards long. It energized me. All that breathing, all those muscles moving in constant harmony. Then I fell asleep for a while.

That night, feeling much better, I was willing to work longer than usual. Luckily, Robert was not coming for dinner.

*

"2. *Proper Nutrition*. To obtain proper nutrition it is not necessary to complicate our lives with confusing numbers such as calorie quantities or with sophisticated and usually dangerous and unbalanced diets that are so common these days. There is a balanced, natural, and simple way to approach foods, easy to learn and practice.

"By learning and practicing this approach to food, we will give our body all the nutrients it needs to feel good and function well.

We will gradually and safely lose all extra weight, become truly healthy, and greatly enhance our immune system. We will feel and look many years younger.

"This way of eating is essentially right for anyone, since we are all made up of the same basic elements. Yet there are some people allergic to certain foods, and this is up to each one of us to find out for ourselves.

"Many people have the erroneous belief that to eat in a healthy, balanced way is dull and unappealing. But this is not so, for when we eat foods in their natural, unprocessed state or properly cooked, we often discover a delightful variety of flavors and textures which most foods have been deprived of by ruthless industrialization, overcooking, and over spicing. The more we experiment with eating natural, unprocessed foods, raw or properly cooked, the more we will experience new enjoyment and pleasure.

"Thus, the simple classification of foods that follows, based on the natural laws of life's evolution on earth, is just a balanced and positive approach to food, allowing us to develop, according to our intuition and taste, many different ways for making it attractive and tasteful.

"*Whole Cereals*. The term 'whole cereal' means grains such as barley, buckwheat, corn, millet, oats, rice, rye, and wheat in their natural, unprocessed, unrefined state. These are the only foods that contain balanced proportions of all the elements our body needs: carbohydrates, fats, minerals, proteins, and vitamins. They are also the cleanest and purest of all foods—purest in the sense that they do not contain any substance negative to our body.

"Unlike any other product of the plant kingdom, grains have both the fruit and the seed in a very concentrated form, full of energy. Unlike any other plant, their tassels grow standing upright, facing the sun, directly purified and charged by its energy. Unlike any other food, they can be stored, under proper conditions, for any period of time without decaying. Some have been found well-preserved in Egyptian tombs.

"When we study mankind's evolution on earth, we learn that all the great civilizations began when man discovered cereals, planted and stored them, and started to eat them regularly. Cereals, as staple foods, have always played a major role in the development of important civilizations.

"Ideally, a good portion of our daily intake of food should be some sort of cereal, by itself or as part of another dish. It's worth mentioning that these are the only foods we can eat daily without our body ever rejecting or getting tired of them.

"But cereals alone are not enough. It's true that their composition is well balanced, but we need some nutrients in greater proportions. Thus, though cereals should be our first choice, they should be supported by other foods.

"It should be made clear that most cereals today are so processed, industrialized, or refined that what we find at most supermarkets or grocery stores has already lost most of its nutritional value. We must find stores where we can get whole grains, whole flours, whole grain breads, whole rolled oats, etc. When we eat white rice, we may be filling up our stomachs but getting very little of the elements our body needs. When natural, whole brown rice is refined into white, it loses most of its nutrients.

"*Vegetables*. The second choice in this balanced, natural way of eating is vegetables. Most have a good nutritional value and are easy to digest but are not as nutritionally balanced nor as pure as cereals. They often have a wonderful flavor and texture and certainly add color and pleasure to our meals.

"A good portion of vegetables should be given to our body every day. They can be eaten raw or slightly cooked—just enough to make them crispy, release their juices, and enhance their taste. When overcooked, vegetables lose most of their nutritional value. We can bake, saute, steam, and make casseroles and pies with them. We can also learn to make different sauces to enhance their taste, yet always keep moderation in mind.

"Especially recommended are broccoli, Brussels sprouts, cabbage, cauliflower, celery, carrots, onions, parsnip, parsley, squash. There are several other vegetables whose composition is a bit imbalanced and should not be eaten regularly, for they will create a measure of disharmony in our bodies. Among these are: asparagus, eggplant, plantain, potato, rhubarb, spinach and tomato. Tomatoes, very acidic and hard to digest, are best eaten cooked.

"*Beans.* High in protein, sweet flavored, and compatible with most foods, beans come third in our balanced, natural way of eating. They should be thoroughly cooked and fulfill a secondary role at meals because they have a high mucus content and require a harder and longer digestion. Therefore, it is preferable not to eat them at the evening meal.

"The whiter they are, the more balanced their composition and the easier to digest. Especially recommended are: chick pea, great northern, lentil, lima, navy, and pinto.

"*Salads.* It is highly recommended to eat some vegetables in their raw state as salads every day. By this we mean all vegetables that can be eaten raw since cooking, especially overcooking, always destroys a significant amount of precious vitamins that are fully preserved in raw vegetables. In addition these foods contain a positive and important amount of minerals.

"Thus, let us get in the habit of eating a good quantity of raw vegetables such as beets, broccoli, cabbage, cauliflower, carrots, lettuce, onions, parsley, watercress, etc., to truly get all the benefits from their nutrients. Gradually include them and others that we might like into our salads. Our body really likes raw vegetables, especially during the season of warm days.

"*Fish.* As most of us know, fish usually has a delicate, fine texture and a wonderful taste. It is also easier to digest and contains more protein than most other animal flesh. Although high in fat, of all animal foods it has the lowest level of toxicity, especially when the flesh is white.

"Fish is an enjoyable, nutritious product that can be eaten regularly.

"*Soups*. On cold days these can be very good and soothing, depending on what they are made of—though too much liquid during meals can disturb an otherwise healthy digestion. Keeping in mind a well-balanced and natural way of eating, we can make our soups thicker and sometimes include a portion of grain.

"*Desserts*. This is one of the most common compensations for anxiety and frustration, and can be very harmful when made with sugar. They do not have a high nutritional value, are very fattening, and 'soften' our system. In other words, they negatively affect our body and mind and bring us down.

"This 'softening of our system' is something that, eventually and distinctly, we will feel and recognize as our body becomes healthier and purer. Moderation is highly recommended regarding desserts, and they should be slightly sweetened, but only with barley malt, fruit juices, raw honey, maple syrup, raisins, or rice syrup.

"*Fruits*. Although most fruits do not have a high nutritional value, some contain vitamins and minerals that are beneficial to our body. It is good to eat fruits regularly, particularly on warm days when our body wants them. It is better for our digestion to eat them before or between meals. When cooked, some of them can be wonderful desserts.

"*Nuts*. Usually high in fats, nuts, except for some protein in a few of them, don't have a high nutritional value. They are not easy to digest and should be very well chewed.

"*Liquid Foods.* The bodily system needs a regular amount of water to perform properly and keep its positive cycle of renewal. Yet, like everything else, liquids should be taken in moderation and slowly, whenever we feel thirsty. Drinking too much will dilute and weaken the elements of our blood stream, making us feel heavy and tired, disrupting the normal pace of our bodily system. As it is only natural to practice a certain balance in everything we do, what we drink should be neither too cold nor too hot.

"A good part of our daily nutrients can be had by taking some foods in their liquefied form—especially a wonderful juice made out of vegetables, full of minerals and vitamins. This way our body does not spend energy in heavy digestion, and afterwards we can easily engage in any other activity.

"It is not advisable to drink during or after meals, as liquids in the stomach disrupt digestion. Pure water, fruit or vegetable juices, and herbal teas are the best beverages. Some products can be combined into wonderful nutritional shakes. Beer, which is made from barley and has a low alcohol content, is less toxic than wine.

"We must be careful with bottled and canned drinks since the majority are produced for profit with not enough consideration for the health of the consumer. Soft drinks full of chemicals and sugar should be totally avoided.

"*Dietary Supplements.* Today most cultivated land has lost much of its minerals and vitamins, so the foods available rarely contain their proper quantity of nutrients. As a result, we rarely get from our foods the necessary elements we need to keep our bodies well. Thus, in most cases, a daily supplement of minerals and vitamins is recommended."

*

In my desire to be as natural as possible, I had sort of rejected taking a daily nutritional supplement or learning more about it. Later, I became more aware of its importance and decided to start taking a complete formula of minerals and vitamins and extra vitamin C.

I feel it is important to point out that our body gets sick or degenerates not only from lack of nutrients, but also from an excess of them. We should be well-informed about the extra nutrients we take.

The day's work was finally over. I felt exhausted and hungry. It was well past our usual dinner time. No calls, no sounds. I cherished silence but felt like listening to some music, sort of having company. I got up to look at the tapes. A while later I went to the kitchen filled with the sound of Mozart's symphony No. 40, so powerful, so uplifting. Bucky got up and followed me. I looked at him; it felt good to have him around.

*

"3. *Negative Foods and Poisons to Avoid.* First, it is necessary to talk about some animal products that contain a certain amount of negativity, the intake of which should be significantly reduced.

"*Dairy Products.* Like other animal foods, dairy products contain hard, saturated fats and cholesterol along with protein; in addition, they produce mucus. Cholesterol collects in our circulatory system, making it increasingly difficult for the blood to flow properly. Mucus collects in our intestines and respiratory system hindering their functions.

"Many of us have noticed how heavy our digestion becomes after we eat a lot of cheese and how sticky our skin seems when we drink whole milk or have ice cream. This toxicity also spreads inside our body. Cow's milk was made by nature for calves, definitely an animal with a biological process very different from that of a man. In any case, the lightest dairy products are skim milk and yogurt.

"The more we reduce our intake of animal products, the better we will feel. We will also lose extra weight because these products contain much more fat than those derived from plants.

"*Eggs*. This commonly consumed animal product has a significant amount of toxicity for it is high in fat and cholesterol and contains too much concentrated protein that the body cannot properly process. In addition, commercially produced eggs contain some of the toxic chemicals given to the hens in order to make them produce more, keep healthy, etc.

"Many of us have felt, particularly in the morning on an empty stomach, the negative influence of eggs which are not easy to digest. Hence, it is better not to eat them regularly, and when eaten, preferably as part of a casserole, pie or cake, they should be counterbalanced with the positive presence of cereals.

"*Canned, Frozen, and Packed Foods*. Most of these foods should also be avoided and their intake reduced as much as possible. Not only have they lost most of their nutrients by overcooking and industrialization, but many colorings, flavorings, and preservatives have been added to them, all poison to the body.

"Now it is necessary to point out some products that should be avoided as much as possible because of their high degree of toxicity. If we look in a dictionary, we will find that the word 'toxic' means poisonous. Thus, every time we consume one of these products, we give our body a certain amount of poison, and the more we use them, the more we poison ourselves.

"These five commonly used products—alcohol, animal flesh, cigarettes, coffee, and sugar—are especially negative because of their high degree of toxicity.

"The toxicity from these products reaches most cells in our body, inflicting a degree of negativity on them, but especially damages the cells which belong to the organ that has been most in contact with it. This gradual infection of the cells causes the already mentioned degenerative diseases such as arthritis, arterio-sclerosis, cancer, diabetes and heart failure, as well as many others.

"Yes, every time we take one of these products, its toxicity will poison our body to a certain degree, and the more we take it, the more our body will suffer the negative effects. Of course, our eyes and skin, the mirrors of our health, will also suffer, get damaged, and show it. But more should be said about each one of them and their very negative toxicity.

"*Alcohol*. This has been a very popular product since time immemorial because it depresses the nervous system to produce an artificial relaxation and a kind of euphoria, and also affects the cells of the brain, suppressing many inhibitions. Yet it increases irrational behavior and decreases alertness, as well as the ability to move properly.

"Alcohol also burns most of the oxygen in our cells, depriving them of the element they need to transform nutrients into energy. This is why when we drink it, the next day we feel worn out, tired, without energy. During the night, our cells could not perform any of their functions properly due to lack of oxygen—especially the function of transforming nutrients into energy or, in other words, creating in our body the proper amount of energy it needs to do well the next day.

"Moreover, we also feel a headache, more or less strong de-pending on the quantity of alcohol we drink. Our brain cells produce this signal of pain as a result of the negative alteration suffered by them.

"Thus, when drinking alcohol becomes a habit, many cells in our body and brain will gradually degenerate, will cease to function properly, and will become easy victims to infection and disease. We will suffer both mental and physical damage.

"The liver, the main cleansing organ of the body, suffers especially from excessive alcohol ingestion as it tries to free the system from its toxicity. A sick, nauseous feeling is the signal given by the overwhelmed, intoxicated organ. Constant alcohol ingestion will eventually poison the cells of the liver causing what is known as cirrhosis of the liver.

"Heavy drinkers usually fail to eat properly, eventually suffering from malnutrition which adds to the weakness of the body and immune system. But the saddest and most tragic result is the overall mental and physical deterioration suffered by them.

"*Animal Flesh*. This is a much consumed product that usually brings with it a high degree of toxicity. Not only is there too much fat containing cholesterol and triglycerides, which are among the main causes of arteriosclerosis, heart failure, and arthritis, but, in addition, there are several kinds of drugs and chemicals given to commercially-raised animals, which are very negative to all the cells of our body. Among these chemicals and drugs are various types of antibiotics to keep them from getting sick, hormones to make them grow faster and fatter, hormones to eliminate their sex drive, pesticides to keep the bugs away, tranquilizers to keep them calm, and God knows what else.

"Arteriosclerosis, or hardening of the arteries, is a negative condition caused by the accumulation of fats on the blood vessel walls that gradually impair the proper circulation of blood. This is a 'whole body' illness that starts with the weakening of our immune system, continues by gradually diminishing our mental faculties and bodily functions, and ends up by clogging our arteries and causing a heart attack.

"The heavy toxicity from all the drugs and chemicals contributes to the causes of various kinds of diseases and negative alterations all over our system such as several kinds of cancer, sexual and reproductive disorders, skin decay, etc.

"Moreover, as animal flesh has no fiber, it is difficult to digest and usually portions of it remain in the intestines, rotting there, a focus of infection, and frequently causing serious illness such as cancer of the colon and acute constipation, among others. A regular cleansing of the colon is highly recommended.

"The excess fat contained by most animal flesh also contributes to obesity, another negative condition which increases mental and physical disorders. Chicken, raised with chemicals like most other commercially-raised animals, is not recommended either.

"Thus, we should avoid animal flesh as much as possible and, when eating it, make sure to balance it with the positive influence of a cereal such as rice, corn, whole breads, etc., for better digestion.

"*Caffeine.* Found in coffee, tea, most chocolates, and soft drinks, caffeine is another popular poison that impairs our senses, mind, and nervous system. It also affects all the cells in our body, especially those in the organs that come in close contact with it.

"Caffeine is addictive, and the first morning cup of coffee satisfies the craving built up by the body during the night. It also stimulates the central nervous system, providing a false sense of energy for a brief period. As the day goes on and we take more caffeine, it will make us nervous, anxious, and restless, impairing positive behavior and causing acute headaches as it intoxicates our brain cells.

"This drug irritates the stomach tissues and promotes secretion of stomach acids, provoking heartburn, ulcers, and cancer. The kidneys, also irritated by caffeine, suffer serious disorders and eventual failure.

"Caffeine is known to cause negative alterations to our circulatory system. It dilates some blood vessels and constricts others. It usually increases our heartbeats and alters our basal metabolic rate, provoking various kinds of internal disorders and impairing the way we act. Naturally, it also contributes to heart disease and various kinds of cancer. It is also linked to fibrocistic breast disease and birth defects.

"It has been found that people who drink several cups of coffee a day have twice the incidence of heart attacks as non-drinkers. It is also a well-known cause of insomnia, impairing a restful, renovating sleep. Excesses of this drug will eventually disrupt our basic bodily functions.

"This is, no doubt, one of the worst poisons taken at present by millions of people.

"*Cigarettes*. These too are one of the greatest poisons and 'downers' of our time. Users are not only intoxicated as soon as they come in contact with them—impairing their mental faculties and senses—but slowly and surely killed by them.

"As soon as the smoke is inhaled, it begins to attack the tissues and continues to do so wherever it goes—mouth, tongue, esophagus, lungs, and stomach. Later, its by-products reach the bladder, pancreas, and kidneys.

"The first dose of nicotine stimulates the brain and the central nervous system, but later doses will make the user nervous and depressed. Like all other toxics, it negatively affects all the cells in our body, especially the most sensitive ones, such as those of the brain.

"Cigarette smoking is a major cause of cancer of the lung, larynx, oral cavity, and esophagus, and contributes to the development of cancer of the bladder, pancreas, and kidney. It is also the major cause of emphysema, a non-cancerous lung disease that gradually destroys the lungs and the breathing capacity.

"Cigarette tar—heavy toxins which are by-products created from the combustion of paper, tobacco, and many solid chemicals used in cigarette processing—has been clearly implicated in overall bodily decay and several serious diseases such as heart and circulatory disease, lung and other cancers, emphysema, and chronic bronchitis. It is estimated that about one quarter of all fatal heart attacks each year are caused by cigarette smoking.

"Nicotine causes blood pressure to rise and increases the heart rate as much as thirty-three beats a minute, reducing blood circulation in the legs and arms.

"The skin, vision, smell, and taste are also damaged by cigarette smoking as the cells that form part of those organs are negatively affected by it.

"It is obvious that people who smoke are not well-balanced, for no one with a healthy mind would bring such harm to their body. They should start by finding out what psychic problems drive them to practice such a terrible habit.

"*Sugar*. 'The white killer,' as many call sugar today, is another highly consumed product that slowly destroys the bodies of the millions of people who consume it daily. It is a sure threat to the health and length of our life.

"This is a pure carbohydrate—it has no other nutrients—made pure by a thorough refinement process. Like refined flour, it causes a negative alteration in the body's metabolism by providing its millions of cells with quick energy without giving them any of the nutrients they need to function properly.

"Yet, to get the energy from refined carbohydrates, our cells must deprive themselves of a good portion of the minerals and vitamins they need to function well and keep our bodies youthfully healthy. This negative chemical process will surely make us old before our time.

"Moreover, bacteria breaks some sugar into acids that dissolve the protective coverings of our molecules, opening the way to further deterioration and decay of all our body structures, organs, and tissues. These acids are so strong that they dissolve the calcium from our tooth enamel, causing acute tooth deterioration and loss.

"Excess sugar is stored in the body as fat, especially in the least exercised areas like the breasts, buttocks, stomach and thighs, then in the major organs such as kidneys and heart, which again suffer deterioration and decay.

"Sugar is one of the major causes of diabetes, heart disease, and circulatory problems. As the major cause of diabetes, it also attacks the pancreas and the liver.

"Unless we are very careful, we might end up taking big daily quantities of this deadly poison. It is not only found in the sugar bowl, infinite kinds of candy and sweets, chocolate, and soft drinks, but also in most canned and packaged foods."

*

Why do so many people eat so many sweets? Because it is a flavor that brings special pleasure, as is obvious from the many fruits people have discovered and planted and made a habit of eating since the very beginnings of prehistoric times, and from the many kinds of 'sweets' they have created since the very beginnings of civilized times.

But, no doubt, most of the people who eat too many sweets do it to compensate for their frustration or distract from their anxiety. Thus, they keep eating more sweets which gradually make them feel more anxious—worse. These people can only solve their problems by finding out the cause of their frustration or anxiety, by finding out what is it that makes them do something so harmful to themselves.

This can also be applied to all those who suffer from any kind of negative habit or addiction. Perhaps they should discuss what makes them victims to negative habits with their psychiatrist or a guru or someone whom they consider wise or maybe even God Itself.

As I finished writing the last message from "the voice," I thought how difficult it must be for most people to follow these recommendations, especially since most of us take little or no care of our spiritual needs and so turn to our bodily needs and sensual pleasures to seek satisfaction. Yes, the majority ignores the fact that the eagerness to drink, to eat and to have too much sex is just a manifestation of the deep anguish that comes from lack of spiritual fulfillment, which can only be appeased by practicing the right activities.

Then what about the people who produce and sell all those enormous quantities of toxic products? For some it is their livelihood, for others, a way to make millions.

It appears that it will take the majority of the human race many more decades to reach higher levels of consciousness and civilization. Will life on our planet—suffering so much destruction due to the fact that most of us have lower levels of consciousness—last that long?

Many more of us should get to know and experience how much better it feels when we give more importance to our spiritual needs than to those of the body or the mind. It's the only way out.

*

"4. *About Meals*. Let us approach food with reverence and thankfulness. It is one of God's most precious gifts. When making a meal, let us handle and cut our food with care and gentleness.

"Let us approach the art of cooking, which is simpler than most think, with care and patience, and discover how creative and interesting it can be. Let us learn to enjoy it; we depend on it for the beauty, health, and youthfulness of our bodies.

"When cooking it is best to use unrefined vegetable oils sparingly—most foods already contain a percentage of fat. Among the best oils are corn, olive, safflower, and sesame. A little butter may be added for taste.

"Let us use condiments in moderation; they can cause imbalances in our bodies and irritate our inner organs. As we eat foods in their natural state or properly cooked, we realize how tasty they are and what little need there is for condiments.

"Eating with moderation is essential to our general well-being. Digesting is a complicated and strenuous task that requires a lot of energy from our body.

"When we overeat, we immediately feel especially clumsy and heavy as our digestion requires a lot of energy and other parts of the body are deprived of it, including the brain. We are overworking our digestive system that, like any other machine, has a limited capacity. These facts alarm our nervous system which, added to the reduced flow of energy in the rest of the body, can make us feel significantly down. We might also add in the negative psychological effect of knowing that we have committed the negative action of overeating.

"Overeating during the evening meal interferes with good restful sleep, for as our body is busy at work digesting a substantial amount of food, and our nervous system is also busy supplying the required amount of energy, our whole being lacks the tranquility required for proper rest.

"In the long run, overeating will gradually deteriorate our digestive system and overtax all the functions of our body, and, logically, these facts will have a negative effect on our general well-being.

"It is recommended to eat slowly just until the moment when we feel gently satisfied.

"Meals are one of the most important parts of our daily lives. On these occasions we give our precious body the material substances it needs to stay in good condition. Not only is the quality of the food or the way we cook it important, but also our approach to it and the circumstances in which we eat it. We should try to eat our meals surrounded by a pleasant and peaceful atmosphere and dedicate the right amount of time just to this activity.

"Let us feel grateful for our food and give thanks to God, even in silence, before each meal. The quality of our bodies and our efforts to become better and happier human beings depends on this food.

"The importance of food to our general well-being cannot be overstressed. Therefore, if we still have unanswered questions, let us keep seeking information until we feel satisfied.

"Today it is difficult to make a choice among the many theories on how to eat right. The only way to know is to try some of them. If we try this one, let us do it gradually, without forcing ourselves, and then let us experience the results."

*

I waited for a while but "the voice" said no more. It had certainly delivered what seemed to be a good classification of foods based on their nature, and much more.

I had experienced a few different ways to approach foods. This one, though similar to one or two of them, I liked better. There is no fanaticism or extremes about it. It feels right. I will call it a "well balanced, mostly vegetarian diet."

I had been writing most of the morning. Though it was not yet noon, I decided to stop. A friend had called to invite me to lunch, but I preferred not to eat in restaurants, and I wanted it to be brief (for the park was waiting), so I told him to come over. We had good leftovers which I could improve.

*

"5. *Proper Exercise*. This is another requirement to be met in order to keep our bodies in good condition—primarily because proper exercise definitely helps to improve and maintain the quality and performance of our muscles and nervous system, and, as a result, it stimulates and enhances our body's vital functions: breathing, digestion, and circulation.

"Moreover, when we exercise, our muscles release a particular enzyme that burns up the fat around them. Thus, if we exercise regularly, we are constantly burning fat throughout our bodily system and creating lean, healthy body mass.

"Therefore, every day we should try to dedicate a certain amount of time to properly activating our bodies, learning to make it an enjoyable habit.

"The basic daily exercises should be those which are most natural to perform. Logically, walking comes first. But walking with balance, energy, and harmony, using our breath as a support and guide, being aware of our movements, aware of the muscles we are using, and doing our best to stimulate them.

"Conscious walking will develop and strengthen the muscles of our legs and lead them to improve their task which will help us to become more grounded and self-assured. This activity is also conducive to setting our bodies and minds in the direction of balance and harmony, as it brings us in touch with our spirit.

"Vigorous walking will also stimulate and enhance our vital functions: breathing, circulation, and digestion, as well as our nervous system. It is a pleasant, undemanding way to benefit our whole body, to observe the world around us, and a good opportunity to practice reflection. Let us walk as much as feels right, with enthusiasm, vitality, and awareness.

"Walking and most other activities will be enhanced by bringing our tongue up and back and placing its lower part against the top of our palate. Thus we will be able to better concentrate on our breathing, which will become more efficient and bring extra well-being into our whole system. Our mouth should be closed.

"Jogging is another good method of stimulating our whole body and exercising our legs and should be performed with the same attitude as we perform walking, its benefits being similar.

"But jogging or running is not a natural form of exercise. It is an activity man does when motivated by special circumstances and requires great amounts of energy. Therefore, it should be done carefully and gently, according to the needs and possibilities of our body, just following our natural rhythm. If overdone, we may suffer an injury and will surely overtax our whole bodily system.

"Similar benefits can also be obtained from bicycling or swimming.

"When we practice any of these activities, it is very interesting and rewarding to observe how our muscles gradually respond to the stimulus and perform increasingly better, as if they had an intelligence of their own.

"Sports like basketball, football, hockey, soccer, etc., if practiced regularly, can be a wonderful substitute for any of the above mentioned exercises.

"It is important to perform all exercises in harmony with the rhythm of the breath. This is the essential factor on which to base and develop any physical activity.

"Definitely, if we want to remain young, healthy, and feeling good, we must exercise regularly.

"There are other, more specialized, forms of exercise to activate and benefit the various parts and functions of our body, such as different kinds of calisthenics and gym workouts. There are others even more specialized and subtle, such as Tai Chi and Hatha Yoga. These are also recommended, but preferably as a complement to one of the more natural forms of exercise mentioned before. Hatha Yoga, especially interesting, will be thoroughly explained in the chapter on the Soul."

*

Exercise. . . . I have always liked to exercise. It has never been a problem for me. I have always enjoyed sports and worked out my body. . . . The more I live and learn, the more I enjoy outdoor activities. They make me feel so good.

It was full moon. Robert was coming early so that after dinner we could go out biking for a while. Of course, Bucky would come with us.

*

"6. *Proper Sleep*. This is a very important part of our daily lives, for it is while we rest that our cells perform most of their functions of maintenance, renewal, and immunity.

"As we lie down resting, especially asleep at night, millions of cells in all the different parts of our body are free to use the energy they need to perform the vital metabolic functions that our body requires to be healthy and do well. They are able to perform the vital functions of processing the nutrients they receive and using the broken-down substances to properly maintain and reproduce themselves and create the necessary amounts of energy we need to properly function the next day. At the same time they activate and keep up a healthy immune system.

"During the day, as we are awake and active, it is our nervous system that uses most of the body's energy to perform all the functions that an active person requires. An active mind requires a lot of energy. The digestive system, while at work, also requires big amounts of energy. And, of course, active muscles and ligaments also spend a lot of energy.

"Proper sleep means sleeping the necessary amount of time that our cells require to perform all their functions. That amount of time varies, depending on our age, between nine and six hours.

"The younger we are, the more sleep we need, because our body is growing, and the cells need to perform extra reproductive functions—our bones, muscles, skin, everything in our body is growing, so our cells need extra energy and time to make that growth happen. Yet, as our body approaches full maturity, we will gradually need less sleep; our cells no longer need the extra amount of time and energy that a growing body requires.

"Sleeping properly also means sleeping from the moment we go to bed to the moment we naturally wake up. If we stay in bed much longer, some of the energy our body has built up during the night will sort of suffocate within, preventing us from feeling really good that day.

"Let us prepare ourselves for a positive and good night's sleep by not going to bed with a full stomach, with our digestive system at work. Let us have the evening meal at least three hours beforehand. Then, when going to bed, let us dedicate a few minutes to prayer and meditation to create a special contact with our spirits and better dispose ourselves to a beneficial sleep."

*

I felt excited by all the wonderful knowledge that came through "the voice." It was an extraordinary fact. I certainly did not know before-hand all that I was writing. It made me feel humble and deeply moved.

Talking about sleep, I had a good one the night before. Our bike ride had been great. At the last moment Adriana called and came to join us. We biked far and easily, discovering the wonderful vegetation of our neighborhood under the moonlit shadows. Playing games with the bikes, joking, teasing each other, behaving like children. Marveling at the mysterious beauty of nature at night.

I remember going to bed lighthearted and smiling.

Let a man be moderate in his eating and his recreation,
Moderately active, moderate in sleep and in wakefulness.

> Krishna, *Bhagavad-Gita*

Wise men eat what the gods leave over after the offering.
But those ungodly,
Cooking rich food for the greed of their stomachs;
Will pay a price,
Their health will suffer, their life much shorter.

> Krishna, *Bhagavad-Gita*

If you give earnest heed to the voice of the Lord,
And do what is right in his sight;
He will put none of the diseases on you,
Which he has put on those who do not obey Him.
For He is the Lord, your healer.

> Moses, *Exodus* 15

And you shall eat in the presence of the Lord your God.

> Moses, *Deuteronomy* 14

He who lives looking for sensual pleasures,
His senses uncontrolled, immoderate in his food,
Will certainly be overthrown,
As the wind throws down a weak tree.

> Buddha, *Doctrine of the Buddha*

If by leaving a small pleasure one attains a great one,
Let's leave the small and have the great.

> Buddha, *Doctrine of the Buddha*

The laws of nature are the laws of health,
And he who lives according to these laws is never sick.

> Jesus, *Aquarian Gospel* 28

When men have learned
That when they harm a living thing they harm themselves,
They surely will not kill,
Nor cause a thing that God has made to suffer pain.

Jesus, *Aquarian Gospel*

Let a man reflect on the food he eats.
How He pours down the rain in torrents
And cleaves the earth asunder;
How He brings forth the corn, the grapes,
The fresh vegetation, the olive, the palm,
The fruit tree and the green pasture,
For you and your cattle to delight in.

Mohammed, *Koran* 86

The Mind

The month of December had arrived. That morning, feeling a little cold, I decided to wear warmer clothes.

A few months before, Robert and I had gone to a dance at a church. It had turned out to be like an aerobics class where most people were dancing by themselves and many doing it in patterns.

But it was a special night, very special. There we met two big, spectacular blondes. One prettier than the other—beautiful figure, beautiful face with big eyes the color of light honey. After the dance we went swimming at a friend's pond and after that she came to our house and remained there for several months.

It was wonderful to have her around, if only to look at. Yet Candy was cheerful, sensitive, vegetarian, very much into exercise, and loved poetry. Soon we started to read and memorize poems together.

The house was suddenly touched by a swift magic wand. Robert and I felt happier and kept everything in better shape. Dinners together became a celebration.

Busy trying to find a job, I had not been writing the last few days. But early that morning, as soon as Candy left to teach one of her dancercize classes, I resumed my very special task.

*

"THE HUMAN BRAIN IS A MAGNIFICENT, natural computer with an enormous potential. It is capable of storing limitless quantities of information in an orderly manner to be released when needed. It can also combine that information so that we can carry out our daily tasks and answer our everyday questions.

"The brain-mind can imagine and wonder all on its own. Thus, it is also a very independent computer, extremely difficult to turn on and off at will. So if it is not somehow controlled, which, as has already been said, is very difficult to do, it works constantly, presenting us with many different thoughts and information. These thoughts can be positive or negative—sometimes so negative that they can easily bring us down and depress us.

"Therefore, how much our brain can help us or bring us down depends on how well we take care of it, control it, and also on the quality of the information it contains. The more positive this information is, the better for us.

"The quality of this information mostly depends upon the atmosphere and the circumstances in which a person grows up. People who grow up surrounded by a positive atmosphere, exposed to positive facts and words, have their brain-computer filled with positive information. They usually have a healthy and optimistic attitude and a better chance to make a constructive and happy experience out of their lives.

"Growing up surrounded by a positive atmosphere is growing up in a household where there is love and order, where parents respect each other and their children, and there is a constructive and harmonious way of life.

"People who grow up surrounded by a negative atmosphere, exposed to various kinds of negative facts and words, store many kinds of negative information in their brain-computer. They are more likely to have a negative and pessimistic attitude and have a greater chance of making a destructive and unhappy experience out of their lives. They are often more inclined to feel down or depressed. This, unfortunately, is the case for many people, the number of whom constantly increases.

"Thus, as we grow up and as adults, our mind is constantly releasing whatever it has in storage, especially when it is not engaged in any constructive activity. Logically, the more negative that information is, the more negative and depressing the thoughts released.

"The strongest negative information stored in our minds is usually some kind of guilt which has gradually built up since childhood. This guilt might be for things we did or thought which were considered very 'bad' according to the standards of older people.

"Low self-esteem, sometimes to an extreme degree, is also the result of negative experiences and information during childhood years. Many other problems, such as difficult friendships and relationships, a pessimistic outlook, professional shortcomings, etc., are the product too of this negative information.

"Some of the absurd concepts taught by some of the great religions, deeply rooted in our brain, are also the cause of much of the guilt that is suffered by many people all over the world. Sometimes we just can't help behaving contrary to these concepts and, as a result, consider ourselves and others guilty sinners. This has caused much of the aggressiveness and confusion that mankind has suffered from for many centuries.

"Moreover, many positive and negative events occur in our daily lives. Every day our brain receives a certain amount of positive and negative information that it processes and stores with greater or lesser intensity, depending on how each piece of that information affects us. This daily information, when combined with whatever we have in storage and when not well processed, can also add to our amount of aggressiveness, anguish, confusion, depression, and sorrow.

"Yes, all that negative information, deeply rooted in our brain-computer, frequently comes out, especially when something considered bad happens to us, usually causing some degree of confusion and depression.

"Therefore, we must seek ways to work with the brain so as to remove its negative information, replace it with positive input, and process new information in a constructive, harmonious way.

"God, the generous, loving and wise Supreme-Universal-Energy that pervades all, has provided us with various ways to achieve this goal.

"The usual way of treating people with moderate mental problems or, in medical terms, various degrees of neurosis, such as anguish, breakdowns, or depressions, is through what has been called psychoanalysis or, in other words, analysis of the mind. There are different ways to apply this approach. Most professionals utilize conversational therapy, though some also include drugs.

"In psychoanalysis the practitioner tries to help the patient understand and realize the negative circumstances or information that caused his or her depression. Once the patient knows the cause of the problem and understands that it is not necessarily an inherent part of his personality, then it will be possible for him to overcome it. Through this method and extra work on self-assertiveness, the practitioner tries to erase from the patient's mind the old negative information and replace it with new, positive information.

"But this way of treating mental disorders completely ignores the important role that the health of the patient's body and the degree of toxicity in his brain cells play in his general well-being.

"To ignore these factors which so much influence a person's behavior not only shows a great deal of ignorance about the integral functioning of human beings, but also prevents any real cure.

"Nevertheless, the frequent conversations, if well-directed, usually help patients understand life and themselves better and add an amount of positive information to their brain storage. In some cases good, extensive therapy can remove some of the deeply rooted negativity and help the patients lead a better life.

"The use of pills that some doctors prescribe may help some people during a critical stage but, if continued, will add to the poisoning of the patient's body and brain, causing more damage than cure.

"Finally, and most importantly, psychoanalysis ignores the natural supremacy of the soul over the mind, without which awareness and acceptance, no human being can ever function in a harmonious way.

"Thus, without the practice of proper nutrition and exercise and some activities to keep in touch with the power of the spirit, no real cure can ever be attained.

"As for the guilty thoughts, first of all, we must realize that most people have had them to a certain extent at some point in their lives. They are usually part of the process of growing up in a confused world, and many have succeeded in overcoming them just by living and comprehending life better.

"If we want to help a particular person, we must begin by learning what kind of guilt the person has. Then we must try to help him or her learn about the origin of the guilty thoughts and the fact that they are not uncommon or unnatural since most people have had guilty thoughts all their lives or at some point in their lives. Finally, he or she must understand the crucial fact that our soul is something absolutely clean and pure, which none of our actions or thoughts can soil or make impure, and that the proper contact with the power and purity of our soul can gradually heal and purify our mind. Yes, understand and learn that it is within one's power to become pure in thought, word, and deed, if one works at it.

"As already mentioned, one of the most common sources of guilt is having negative thoughts about our parents, sometimes even to the point of hating them. This is easily understandable, since it is they who, by their example and words, are responsible for most of the basic information that has been in our brain since childhood. And it is this information which largely determines our successful or unsuccessful adjustment to living in a complex world. It is this information which plays a very important role in our success or failure in life.

"Therefore, many of us consider our parents responsible for much of the unhappiness we suffer and thus can harbor many negative thoughts relating to them. These thoughts can create heavy guilt and bring us way down—for, supposedly, to think in such a way about our parents is very unnatural and wicked. Yet it is common and natural."

*

As usual, what ever came out of my writing sessions made me think and ponder. Especially all the concepts about guilt and negative information.

Somehow it all made sense. I knew very well how an uncontrolled mind is usually the source of most of our problems. I had dealt with mine for many years, sometimes, I think, almost to the point of losing the battle. Thanks to prayer and the constant practice of proper nutrition, exercise, and other activities to keep in touch with the guidance and power of my spirit, I found direct contact with "It" that has gradually led me to ever higher levels of consciousness and well-being.

That afternoon there would be no park for me. Adriana had asked me to come with her downtown. She had to take some photographs for one of her courses and did not want to do it alone.

*

"ONCE WE UNDERSTAND THAT THE BRAIN-COMPUTER-MIND is just an excellent biological machine with a high degree of independence, we will start taking good physical care of it—that is, keep it clean (no toxins) and give it proper fuel (good nutrition). Then we should gradually lead our mind to consider the world around us in a positive and realistic way by constantly providing it with positive and realistic information. Finally, we must find a way to keep our computer-mind under reasonable control.

"Yes, our brain-computer, unlike man-made computers, can, through the right natural process, gradually renew itself and change old knowledge into new. Ultimately, at its highest state, it can place itself under the constant ascendancy of the soul. Although a fascinating process, it takes discipline, effort, and patience. Yet the rewards are marvelous; there is no better experience in life, and it relates to all we do.

"The following method of dealing with the mind is effective, simple, and easy to understand. If practiced, it will be of great help in the gradual process of making our brain-computer-mind a harmonious component of our being.

"1. *Proper Breathing*. This is one of the most important factors in the process of bringing the mind into a state of harmony and positivity and keeping it there.

"First of all, proper breathing will bring sufficient oxygen to our brain cells, enabling them to properly process and use the nutrients they receive and thus to function better.

"Moreover, when our body receives the amount of oxygen it needs, the nervous system remains tranquil. Otherwise, it will constantly send warning signals to our brain causing nervousness or stress, diverting the mind from its rightful focus of attention, creating or increasing anguish. Logically, under these circumstances we become unable to concentrate properly and to satisfactorily perform any kind of activity.

"Furthermore, in the moments when we are not performing any kind of activity, we should concentrate on breathing properly and on its pleasant rhythm. This will help keep our mind calm, bring positive thoughts, and prevent negative ones.

"It is highly recommended to concentrate ourselves as often as possible on the natural and pleasant task of proper breathing.

"2. *Proper Nutrition and Exercise*. It seems necessary to repeat that the food we eat has an enormous influence on our brain cells. It determines the amount and balance of necessary nutrients that these cells receive through our circulatory system. This in turn determines to an important degree the balance and harmony of our mind.

"Unless we practice the right approach to foods we will never attain higher degrees of consciousness and really enjoy and understand life.

"It is important to mention that the way we eat the evening meal—how heavily or lightly, balanced or unbalanced—will determine, to a significant degree, how heavy or light, balanced or unbalanced we feel the following day. Similarly, what we eat in the morning will influence in a positive or negative way the general feeling of the day, and so on.

"In other words, what we eat has an immediate influence on how we feel. It can make us feel high or down, good or bad in a matter of minutes.

"Proper exercise is also highly recommended to help improve the state of our brain cells. It brings extra amounts of oxygen to our cells, resulting in their better functioning and well-being. It helps prevent negative thoughts from entering our minds as we concentrate on a positive activity.

"3. *Proper Sleep*. To have a good, restful sleep is of extreme importance to the successful functioning of the mind. First of all, it is when we sleep that the brain cells, as well as those of the rest of the body, perform their functions of maintenance and renewal and create the required amount of energy to function properly the next day. Thus, the better we sleep, the better our mind will perform the following day. This is a normal occurrence that all of us should have experienced.

"Equally important is the fact that it is mostly during a good night's sleep that our brain cells perform their function of processing and firmly establishing the knowledge that we have acquired or grasped the day before. In other words, it is mostly at night during sleep that the brain-computer processes new knowledge and makes sure it is added to its vast storage.

"Surely some of us have noticed that when we have been learning something new, be it intellectual or physical, we often discover ourselves correctly understanding concepts or performing actions that we did not understand or do well the day before.

"Thus, sleeping properly is of extreme importance to the successful functioning of the mind. Let us do our best to prepare ourselves for a good night's sleep.

"4. *Be active all day.* To keep ourselves constantly busy with constructive or creative activities is an excellent way to prevent the mind from dwelling on negative thoughts. Of course, we need to take the necessary breaks to properly balance our day.

"5. *Increase the amount of daily positive information.* Let us read only serious or uplifting newspapers and publications, watch only highly educational and instructive television programs in order to feed our computer-mind with positive information. Let us not believe everything we read or everything we listen to on the radio or watch on television. Let us be aware of the fact that very few people that work or express themselves in the media have a high level of consciousness.

"Watching too much television is extremely negative. Not only are we giving our mind high amounts of negative information and entertainment and losing precious time that could be used in uplifting activities, but we are also receiving small amounts of radiation harmful to our bodies.

"Let us associate and socialize with constructive and positive people so as to give our minds more positive information on this level also.

"Let us avoid gossip and idle talk. To spread negative information creates negativity, especially for the person who does it. Let us avoid talking about the negative side of things; we do not want to increase or solidify the negative information our mind already has. We do not want to spread or solidify negative information in the world around us.

"6. *Improve language habits*. Words are a significant expression of man's evolution on earth. They clearly show our individual process of evolution and our present level of consciousness. Thus, to enhance our own process, let us learn to avoid vague and vulgar words; let us learn to express ourselves clearly and pronounce carefully.

"Let us be increasingly aware of what we think and say, and learn to recognize when our words come from the heart—sincerely, spontaneously—and when they come from the mind—calculating, induced by selfish interest. That is, let us learn to recognize when our words convey positivity and when they convey negativity.

"7. *Learn by heart a positive sentence*. This practice can be quite beneficial to those who feel attracted to do it. It can help us improve the way we feel and our present approach to life.

"When we make a positive sentence and firmly store it in our mind, we can use it any time to bring us positivity and good feelings.

"We can say it aloud every morning, being sure to convey its meaning. We can also say it whenever we feel like it, especially when negative thoughts come to our mind.

"We can make our own sentence or choose one of the following:

"Every day in every way I am getting better and better.
God knows better and wants the best for me.
I can learn to perform as well as the best.

I shall live this day with love in my heart.
From my mistakes I shall learn to improve my life.
Life can be wonderful, it depends on me.
Today I begin a new life."

*

Life had become wonderful. It was a real pleasure to have Candy around. Her beautiful person in the kitchen making her healthy shakes. Her beautiful eyes looking at me, smiling. Her child-like voice saying sweet and funny things.

I had learned to recognize the sound of her car and often expected to hear it at any moment. She had no set schedule in her comings and goings.

That night it was my duty to cook. I was learning to do it better; it was motivating to do it for others. Pinto beans and brown rice were already on the stove as I sat down to continue writing down my magical communication with "the voice."

*

"8. *Prayer.* Every morning, preferably after a shower, we should dedicate a few minutes to prayer—just to practice this beautiful and uplifting activity in both of its forms, spontaneous or traditional, in whichever order feels best.

"Spontaneous prayer is just saying whatever we feel to our loving Father-Universal-Energy or to an image of any of the great masters or saints which can represent to us God-Itself. This is one of the highest and surest ways to communicate with our Father-God and to establish a beautiful and rewarding relationship with It. It is also one of the best ways to release anxiety or stress.

"This kind of prayer will surely help us, as we listen to those spontaneous words coming from within, to find out what we really want and to become aware of our present degree of consciousness. Yes, being aware of our attitudes and listening to ourselves during these very sincere moments will reveal, to a great extent, our present degree of confidence, faith, love, purity, selflessness, etc., and the contrary—ambition, envy, greed, insecurity, selfishness, etc.

"Thus we will learn to recognize when our words come from our selfless soul, our hearts, and when they come from our selfish minds. That is, it will help us realize our actual state of positivity or negativity—a constructive and interesting realization.

"Moreover, this daily practice will give our minds a lot of positive information, for what we ask or say as we pray will gradually become clearer, more sincere, more from our true nature. So, as the mind listens, it will realize and store a lot of precious information that comes from our hearts, from that infinite source of love, power, purity, and righteousness that we have inside. This daily process will certainly help us erase a lot of negativity from our computer minds.

"Spontaneous prayer is no doubt one of the most effective tools to help control the mind and gradually take it into the state of harmony that will bring us to happiness and well-being.

"Traditional prayer is another wonderful way to achieve a positive uplift. By daily repeating any well-known prayer that we like, or one of the beautiful parts of the Sermon on the Mount, or the *Bhagavad Gita* or the *Koran*, we will receive a precious amount of very positive and pure information that our brain will gradually and firmly store. The well-known, great masters—Krishna, Moses, Buddha, Jesus and Mohammed—having reached higher levels of consciousness, are an invaluable source of divine and positive information.

"As we say these precious words, trying to understand and convey their meaning, we will increasingly benefit and enjoy them. We will realize that they, indeed, communicate very important facts.

"Every day, preferably two or three times, we should practice, to our enormous benefit and pleasure, some spontaneous and some traditional prayer. Just being ourselves, just doing it the way we feel."

*

I had already practiced the wonderful activity of prayer for years. I had realized long ago how positive, powerful, and enjoyable it can be. I had discovered that by saying what I really felt I could certainly communicate with my Father, feel higher, and expect good results.

Due to my contact with Christianity since early childhood, I had the habit every morning of saying a famous traditional prayer, the "Our Father." However, I modified it a little; I do not like the way it places God above and far away from us when it says: "Our Father who is in heaven." So I changed it to: "Our Father who is within us and everywhere."

I also felt like eliminating the word "evil." I did not want to think about and repeat every day such a strong and negative word. So instead of saying "and deliver us from evil," I changed it to "and deliver us from negative actions."

Yes, prayer has been a wonderful habit, perhaps the most important factor on my hopefully successful journey towards becoming a real human being.

*

"9. *Meditation*. This is a very effective way to bring the mind under control and into harmony. To meditate is to concentrate on something so as to stop the never-ending thinking process, just trying to concentrate for a certain period of time—ideally fifteen minutes to half an hour.

"Daily practice of meditation will help us control the endless, often disharmonious, thinking process of a negative, wandering mind. It will keep the mind from functioning when it is not needed and gradually train it to get in tune. It is also an excellent way to become aware of a negative thinking process and escape from it for a while to a state of peace, quiet, relaxation.

"After a few years of daily practice—the amount of years depends on each individual process—the mind will gradually tune in to God's guidance, and our natural state will become one of conscientious activity, enthusiasm, harmony, inner peace, and happiness.

"Meditation is also a very good method of processing information in a positive way, particularly for those who are confused or have doubts about different matters.

"For some reason thoughts and questions that we have, things that we fear, positive or negative memories, tend to appear off and on during meditation. All this information is clearly understood, well-processed, and properly dismissed or stored by some special inward process. We will usually come up with the right answer to our questions, gradually release the negativity, and end up with a positive attitude.

"A deeply rooted piece of negative information will take longer to process, but eventually we will process it and become free of it.

"When we practice meditation and make it part of our lives, we also have the privilege of enjoying, every day, the most wonderful refuge, the best place to relax and renew ourselves. There we will encounter a realm of clarity, harmony, and love. Let us do it and find out for ourselves.

"There are, however, different techniques of meditation, different schools, different ways to help us concentrate on something. Many teachers have taught various forms of meditation or various ways of approaching the same technique.

"It is very important for us to find the best one, the one that feels most comfortable and natural. Then the process of bringing the mind into harmony will evolve better and faster. Yet we have to be careful and sensitive in our search for the most convenient kind of meditation. We must carefully sense which one feels best.

"Meditation is so important and personal that it is hard to advise any particular method. It is something that each person should find out for himself. It has to be a genuine and sincere search following the advice of our hearts, our souls, our purest source of truth. Yet it seems right to point out that concentrating on our breathing process is the kind of meditation most appropriate for the majority of people. This subject will be further explained in the next chapter.

"10. *Work at suppressing the Ego.* This is a term used by modern psychiatry to define one aspect of our personality. It can also be considered the negative, selfish, uncontrolled thinking of an independent mind.

"Suppressing the ego is simply trying to do what we have been talking about all along—to control and gradually suppress the independent, negative thinking process of the mind. It is one thing to be ourselves, to be a real person, and another to have a strong ego, to be a self-centered and selfish person. A strong and highly developed ego often brings loneliness, misery, and sometimes even death.

"People with a strong ego, even if they are materially successful, are commonly unhappy, try to draw attention to themselves, often turning to extremes and rarely understanding the cause of their unhappiness. Ego, our worst enemy because it blinds us to what is best in life, will gradually disappear if we practice as well as we can what is recommended for the body, the mind, and the soul.

"Let us be more aware of our thinking processes in order to realize when selfish thinking is happening. Let us try to understand and realize that we are all the same, that no man is an island; that we are just a small part of the evolutionary process of the Universe; that there is nothing we can do without the help of God."

*

This part about the ego definitely touched me; I once had a very strong ego. No doubt many of us do, until we start receiving hard lessons from life and hopefully understanding that we are just part of a whole and that we are all, more or less, very similar.

Anyway, my ego, like most others, developed for the usual reasons: the negative effect of the upbringing by immature parents and the negative effect of cultural influence. This made me very selfish and narrow-minded and, as a result, unhappy for a considerable period of my life. It's taken me many years of constant effort to get rid of it and to increasingly realize that whatever good I do is only thanks to God, and that only by communing, giving and sharing with others can a man reach true happiness.

This afternoon was more than pleasant—it was significant. I biked to the park slowly, observing the well-kept gardens, enjoying the beauty around me, and memorizing Edgar Alan Poe's poem "Annabel Lee"—so romantic, so sad. This gave me one of the highest and happiest times ever. I remember crying out of joy and feeling I was surely on the right track.

Again, I strongly realized how dealing with poetry makes me grow, makes me feel better.

I loved the vegetation in Miami—so green, so lush and yet not overwhelmingly tropical. The Banyan trees, so strong, so generous, exuberant—some of their roots stood up in the air as though trying to exist to the fullest . . . many so absolutely spectacular.

*

"11. *Poetry.* Let us read aloud, memorize, recite poems or songs of a spiritual nature. This is a wonderful and pleasant way to learn new things about life, to add positive information to our brain-computer, and to keep erasing negative, old information.

"Writing poetry and songs from our highest spiritual source is an activity from which no one can expect to make money. There-fore, it is something to be done with pure and sincere intentions. It comes from a very pure source, the soul, without contamination from the negative part of the mind. Thus, any such poem that we carefully read aloud or memorize will give us information of the highest quality and make us feel better.

"As we experience poetry, we can enjoy and acquire a very refined, interesting, and valuable knowledge. It is such an enjoy-able way to discover and learn new things and points of view that we will surely make it part of our lives. It is not only a source of wonderful knowledge, but also of the highest feelings and experi-ences, concentrated in a few words from the souls of people who have often developed a high degree of awareness—people, basi-cally like all of us, with a body, a mind, and a spirit.

"Poetry should be read aloud. When read in silence, particu-larly if we have any problems, it is not easy to concentrate on it or to really understand and digest it. When reading aloud, not only our eyes will help us concentrate and digest, but also our ears. This way we have a better chance to get involved in what we read and truly understand and retain that information, a better chance to realize and comprehend what the author was trying to express and make his experience almost our own.

"As we memorize a poem, learning a small part each time, we will find more meaning in its words and understand it better. It will gradually yield more of whatever it has to say. We will absorb and retain even more of its high, positive information and keep discov-ering new aspects of the world around us through the author's different point of view and sensitivity. Then, as we accept and retain this new and positive information, our brain-computer will automatically erase more of the old negative information.

"When we get to know a poem by heart and recite it, the positive process continues, as well as the pleasure and the good feelings. Moreover, we will have something beautiful and valuable to share with others.

"Poetry definitely enriches our perception and understanding of the materiality and spirituality of life, helping to increase our knowledge in a wonderful way as we raise our level of consciousness. We can get very high with poetry, in every sense—a great deal more than we imagine."

*

Poetry,
Divine expression of the soul.
Creation,
That when coming from the right source
Flourishes spontaneously,
Sometimes to unknown and enormous
And divine dimensions.

Language of the soul.
Language of the love that dwells inside us all,
Language of the real you and the real me.
Poetry,
Magic, sublime, unique, divine.

I wrote this poem, "Language of the Soul," for a poetry workshop that I attended at the New School in New York City.

I read and wrote a few poems when I was very young. But it was Martin, my younger brother, man of the world, lover of life, sensitive poet, to whom I feel very grateful for really opening me up to the magical world of poetry. Now, resting in peace, he is always with me.

*

"12. *Music*. This, one of the most obvious manifestations of man's creativity, has been happening all over the world from the beginnings of civilization.

"In one way or another mankind has always been creating music. It has been coming out of our souls with strength and variety. It has been a common and spontaneous way through which men have successfully tried to turn their minds away from negative thoughts and come into contact with their souls and God.

"Yes, listening to music or making music with any kind of instrument, is another wonderful way to keep negative thoughts away from our minds and come into closer contact with our souls. But how effectively it will prevent negative thoughts and bring us closer to our spirits, depends on the music we listen to or the music we make.

"There are marked distinctions among all the different kinds of music created by men. They express many different cultural backgrounds, many different levels of sensitivity or consciousness. Man's source of creativity can be closer to his senses than to his soul. Thus, some music can arouse our senses or bring about negative thoughts, while some can bring us closer to our souls and to high and beautiful feelings.

"The music of the highest quality is usually the so-called religious music that is commonly played in churches, monasteries, temples, etc. Classical music, composed by men with high levels of consciousness and sensitivity, is also of a very high quality. Both kinds of music, divinely inspired, are often created by the same composers.

"There are many other forms of music, varying in quality, composed by many different kinds of men with lower levels of consciousness and sensitivity. There is a great variety of it.

"Therefore, if we want to try to keep negative thoughts away with the help of music and bring ourselves to higher levels of sensitive experience, it is preferable to listen to religious or classical music.

"Let us learn to listen or make music of the highest quality so as to experience the highest feelings, the highest pleasure. Like everything else, enjoying the highest music can be learned. The more we listen to it, the more we get used to it, the more we enjoy it. It is very simple.

"The magic of music—usually exciting, sometimes fantastic—is right there at our disposal, just waiting for us to explore its infinite variety and richness. Let us enjoy it and get high with one of life's greatest treasures."

*

God, how can I forget those many lonely evenings spent trying to avoid negative thoughts with the beauty and power of Wagner's flowing, sometimes ecstatic music. . . . Comforted by it, inspired by it, and thinking that, somehow, if he had the inspiration and talent to create and enjoy such music, many of us could also have the potential to create other things. Yes, feeling hope from thinking that if men can create such music, we surely have the potential to be marvelous creatures.

How can I forget the many evenings spent listening to the brilliant, magnificent, and unique voice of Maria Callas, pouring out her divine soul through her marvelous art—highest source of beautiful feelings, inspiration, and strength. . . .

With his heart serene and fearless,
Holding the mind from its restless roaming,
Let him struggle to reach my oneness,
His highest prize, his life's purpose.

Krishna, *Bhagavad-Gita*

Make a habit of practicing meditation
So to keep your mind from disturbing,
Thus you'll finally come to the Lord,
The light giver, the highest of the high.

Krishna, *Bhagavad-Gita*

As a bowman makes straight his arrow,
A wise man makes straight
His trembling and unsteady thought,
Which is difficult to guard, difficult to hold back.

Buddha, *Doctrine of the Buddha*

Those who bridle their mind,
Which travels far and moves about alone,
Will be free from the bonds of the tempter.

Buddha, *Doctrine of the Buddha*

The concepts derived from the mind
Are not as important
As the images aroused by the Word.

Buddha, *Doctrine of the Buddha*

Words are naught
Till they are made alive,
Until the lessons they contain
Become a part of head and heart.

Jesus, *Aquarian Gospel* 28

Indeed man transgresses
In thinking himself his own master,
For to our Lord all things return.

> Mohammed, *Koran* 96

Their hearts are sealed;
They are devoid of understanding.

> Mohammed, *Koran* 63

By the sun and his midday brightness,
By the moon, which rises after him,
By the day, which reveals his splendor,
By the night, which silently veils him.

> Mohammed, *Koran* 91

The Soul

That period of my life in South Miami was definitely wonderful. Our house, surrounded by a large space of grass and trees, was in an area where most other houses were also surrounded by large spaces of well-kept vegetation. It was a pleasure to walk or bike around . . . all one could see was beautiful and pleasant, many varieties of green and flowers.

December went by without my doing much work with the book. My mother came to visit from South America and stayed with us. We all did our best to make her feel good and enjoy her stay. Then other friends I wanted to see and spend time with also came. Finally, I felt like participating in some of the events that come with the celebration of Christmas.

We all had a good time, but now it was over. Another January had arrived, and we were back to our more tranquil, but also enjoyable, daily and weekly routine.

I had been missing my work with the book. It had become such an interesting and significant part of my days. I felt that besides learning and being reassured by precious knowledge, I was doing something important for humanity. It was exciting to work at it.

The morning finally came when I was ready again, eagerly expecting to hear about the soul. It seemed to me, at the moment, the most important subject.

*

"HUMAN BEINGS HAVE A SOUL—Divine Energy within, precious part of the all-pervading God, Creator and Sustainer of Universal Harmony. Being part of God, our soul is in direct and permanent contact with It, always one with It, always under Its guidance, and ready to take us to ever higher levels of beauty, creativity, harmony, and love.

"We are also part of the universe, all of us evolving in the seemingly endless universal evolution. Yet each one of us was created to play a definite part in that constant happening, that constant universal change. Each one of us was placed into this world to play a particular role—our individual, natural way of being and doing, no matter how unimportant it may seem. And it is only when we understand and fulfill this role that we can positively evolve in this life—feeling good, constantly learning about ourselves and life, and reaching ever higher levels of consciousness and contentment.

"Although most people don't know it, man feels the highest pleasure and fulfillment whenever he lives according to this guidance from within. Thus, to live according to this guidance is the highest purpose in a man's life.

"In other words, to really get to be ourselves, feel good, and experience ever increasing joy, real success, and peace of mind, we must follow the guidance from within; we must be a manifestation of our souls; we must live according to our individual natural duty.

"This inner guidance is very subtle, but constant and strong. If we do not follow it, we become victims of anguish, frustration, nervousness, sadness; we experience "stress." If not remedied, this condition will gradually lead us to sickness of body and mind—a gradual and subtle self-destruction, simply because we are not true to ourselves.

"It can be said that to follow the guidance of our souls is to follow our deep inner feelings, feelings in the highest sense of the word. This does not mean obeying our senses or sexual instincts, but rather obeying feelings that come from within, from the heart, sort of a deep and pure intuition. The more we follow it, the better we feel; the less we follow it, the worse we feel.

"In sum, the only way to feel really good is to live according to the guidance of our souls, and this is the highest purpose in a man's life; this is to be 'one with God.'

"Yet to follow this guidance from within and behave accordingly is very difficult. First of all, most of us do not know that we have such a magnificent source of knowledge within. Then, few of us have the self-assurance or the courage to follow these precious feelings when most others and our own reasoning often say the contrary.

"Since childhood, most of us have been encouraged to ignore what we really feel. It is not easy to believe a voice that comes from within when we have always been told to believe something else, when our brain-computer-minds have long been overwhelmed with information telling us not to be ourselves.

"Yes, since childhood, our minds have been filled with all kinds of information designed to fulfill the requirements of the body and the senses but giving little consideration to the needs of the spirit, regarded as useless in terms of making a living.

"But even in obtaining material stability, it is an advantage to have peace of mind and feel centered, for then we will have the freedom to really dedicate ourselves to any activity.

"Moreover, many people live ignoring the fact that the most successful and satisfying way to make a good living, even if, in some cases, it may take longer, is to follow the guidance of our souls, our vocation. For only then we will be doing what we do best and sooner or later achieve material success. But, more importantly, we will be doing what we enjoy, what we really like, with the positive results that such a situation brings—spiritual harmony and material stability.

"Yes, in a world pervaded with such an overwhelming materialism and often inharmonious activity, it is very difficult to be clear as to who we really are or what we really want. It is very difficult to be our real selves and follow that subtle voice from within.

"Poor humanity. So full of aggression, anger, frustration, and unhappiness. Poor suffering beings that crowd mental hospitals, go to psychiatrists, drag their bodies around in sadness and despair unaware of the cause of their suffering. Unaware that, in most cases, it all happens simply because they are far from being themselves or do not have the courage to be themselves.

"There is so much alarm, so much research, talk, and writing about this so-called stress, which is just anguish and sadness caused by lack of fulfillment of individual spiritual needs and by not being true to ourselves.

"Moreover, there is the sad tragedy of so many children, teenagers, and adults who turn to the destructive nightmare of drugs, mostly because they are simply trying to escape from their anguish and confusion caused by the same unavoidable struggle— the confrontation of their natural, pure, and true feelings with the strong and often incorrect concepts and values of the outside world.

"They are the unfortunate victims of concepts and values to which they confusedly yield—values that usually originate in the teachings of well-meaning but so often aggressive, confused, immature, unhappy parents—towering figures whom we are supposed to believe and respect.

"Bewildered children and teenagers turn to drugs or aggressiveness for relief, unable to grasp that the main problem is that the outside world does not live up to the right standards, does not give them a good chance to be their real selves—the happy and harmonious human beings they were created to be.

"Yes, human beings have both material and spiritual needs which should be fulfilled in a balanced, natural way. Many people today, especially in the big cities, are not living up to this essential, natural requirement, not living what they really feel. Instead, they go against their individual, natural drive and, as a result, become angry, confused, depressed, frustrated, and sad—manifesting all that negativity around them. Yet they only need to understand that they have a soul and that they should try to follow its guidance, at least to a certain degree.

"Fortunately, we never lose the capacity to feel and know our souls and follow their guidance. It is always there within, subtle but strong, just waiting to be felt and followed, just waiting to lead us from darkness into light. Yes, our soul is constantly trying to make us aware of the best approach to life, constantly trying to do all it can to lead us to higher levels of consciousness along the path to creativity, enthusiasm, freedom, peace of mind.

"But when our bodies are clumsy, heavy, poisoned by bad food, or suffering from health problems; when our brain cells are poisoned, and we suffer from headaches, insomnia, or nervousness—then it is almost impossible to pay heed to the constant but subtle advice of our divine soul. We have no choice but to live angry, confused, frustrated, and sad, and to finally die in despair and bewilderment. To finally die unaware of the cause of our tragedy, unaware that we went through life like half-dead beings, confused, following the often contradictory and negative advice of the outside world. To finally die never having been our real selves nor having experienced beautiful levels of consciousness, freedom, peace, or well-being.

"Yes, so many of us go through life in such a sad way, when it could be such an exciting and wonderful adventure. So many of us go through life far from knowing who we really are, what life is all about, helpless victims of anger, envy, and frustration. Like machines, poor, heartless robots dragging our sick bodies here and there, living deadly ignorant of the truth, and poor slaves to unspontaneous, confused minds and ever hungry senses. Prisoners for life in relentless misery."

*

What just came out was very strong; it made me feel worried and sad. Do so many people really live in negative darkness?

Yes, I guess they do; there are so many manifestations of negativity around—so many people having children that they cannot raise properly, so many unwanted children, so many abortions, so much negative and unnecessary sex. Everywhere in the world, there is ever more construction of commercial and residential buildings and roads, and destruction of the natural environment. Ever more unnecessary products that create alarming quantities of garbage and pollution. Ever more distractions that divert us from what we really are, from what we really enjoy.

Why? What causes all this blind, negative materialism? Is it greed? Yes, it must be greed. But greed is the result of insecurity and fear—insecurity and fear due to ignorance of the security and courage that comes when one lives pursuing the true purpose of life. So I guess ignorance is the root of all this chaos.

Is it too late? Is it too late for mankind to evolve just enough to stop the on-going, very alarming, and rapidly approaching destruction of life on our planet?

*

"THANK GOD THERE ARE WAYS TO OVERCOME to a great extent all that negativity and gradually reach higher states of positivity. To show mankind how to do this, our Father Supreme Universal Intelligence has created, since very ancient times, special men whose task has been to teach others that there is only one God, that they have a soul, that their soul is in direct and permanent contact with God, and that their soul is constantly telling them what to do, even regarding small and apparently unimportant matters.

"These men also affirm that when we start living according to our souls advice, our anguish and worries will gradually disappear, that the closer we follow that guidance, the happier and better we will feel, that eventually we will become beings of light, inspiring others by our behavior and example, improving the world around us and experiencing constant well-being. Finally, in order to attain those higher levels of consciousness and well-being, they teach specific activities that we can practice in order to get in closer contact with our souls—in sum, the exciting adventure of living, pursuing the highest purpose of life.

"Yes, our Creator has been creating these great teachers since time immemorial just to convey to other men the real purpose of life. But the essence of their teaching has mostly been lost. Most of their followers have developed limited, oppressive religions, some of which have become instruments of material gain and political power, often bringing terrible divisions, hatred, and war among mankind.

"Many of the concepts and actions of the past and present leaders of these religions represent a great departure from the original teachings of the great masters. These teachings have consisted mainly of a daily practice to attain higher degrees of consciousness and harmony as we get closer to God's guidance, so that we can experience brotherhood, love, unity, and well-being."

*

A few days had passed since I had interrupted my writing. Among other things, I had to make some money to take care of my bills. Sometimes I received money from my family, but not regularly.

That morning I was not feeling good. The night before I had overeaten and, as a result, I did not have a proper rest. Overeating was still one of my problems, one of the few things that sometimes would prevent me from having a good day.

During the long years in my quest to reach a higher quality of life, I have been gradually trying to control or balance some of the so-called pleasures of the senses. With some, it has just happened naturally, for as I evolved and felt better, they simply lost their powerful attraction. With others it has been much more difficult, especially with sugar and coffee, both of which have been arduously testing my will power and mind control.

Overeating, especially at night, was far from being subdued. It angered and worried me, for I clearly felt its negative effects. But I had learned to have patience, and, once one really is on the path to reach higher levels of consciousness and realizes how much better life becomes, one has no choice but to continue making the effort and learning to enjoy it.

Someday, I was sure, overeating would also gently disappear from my life. But it was time to come back to the soul; I could not wait to keep learning about it.

*

"THERE HAVE ALWAYS BEEN RELATIVELY UNKNOWN masters that have also taught the knowledge of Truth, though they were not destined for worldly recognition. Therefore, this knowledge has been constantly taught on earth since time immemorial, and human beings have always had the chance to learn about it.

"Some people say: 'Yes, the truth is one, but there are many paths to reach it.' This may be right, but, if we follow the established and proven methods of the Great Masters, we are sure to get there, or very near, much sooner. It just makes more sense to take the clearest, proven paths than to take deceiving short cuts that may lead to dead ends and loss of precious time.

"After a few years of studying, experiencing, and understanding the essential teachings of the Great Masters, we will realize that it can basically be reduced to the practice of six different activities. These beautiful and enjoyable activities, developed through centuries of practice and evolution, will bring us into direct contact with our soul, God within, the purest, most perfect, and strongest source of energy, knowledge, love, understanding and well-being.

"Yes, through the practice of these activities we will realize who we really are and what we really want. We will gradually be able to follow the guidance of God and do whatever we were created to do. All anxiety and negativity will progressively disappear as every new day, every new week, we understand life better and feel higher.

"Thus, to reach the highest goal, we must develop the daily practice of some of these activities. The more of them we practice the better. The more we systematically include them in our daily lives, the sooner we will reach our wonderful object.

"But this process cannot be forced. It should happen out of understanding and willingness. It should gently fit into our daily lives and gradually become a pleasurable habit. We should do it with care, patience, and moderation, just trying to really concentrate and let it happen, flowing with it, learning to enjoy it more and more.

"Since it is one of the major purposes of this work to present the common origins and similarities of the great teachings and religions of the world, it is important to point out that, as far as is known, it was the founders of Hinduism who, for the first time, organized these precious activities into the basis of a religion that was to become one of the most significant in mankind's evolution. Yet, even before Hinduism existed, these activities had been at the core of all the great civilizations. For only thanks to them men became gradually civilized and able to create and develop significant achievements and cultures. Moreover, since these activities are definitely the teaching of the Universal Spirit God, most men have in their hearts a deep feeling and yearning for them.

"Yoga—which in Sanskrit, the language of ancient India, means 'Union with God'—is the name given to these spiritually oriented activities since the beginning of Hinduism. Thus, to perform one of them means to try to achieve union with God through the practice of that particular activity. Here they will be presented using their English and Sanskrit names which is appropriate to the general purpose of this book."

*

I felt good. I felt very happy with what was coming out. This knowledge is going to help a lot of people.

Suddenly, the lake and Candy swimming in her black bathing suit came to my mind. How much I enjoyed that.

There was quite a nice lake in our neighborhood, surrounded by big homes and their beautiful gardens. One day, Candy and I discovered a path, hidden among trees and bushes, that led to one end of it. After that we got into the wonderful habit of going there to swim as often as we could.

I guess the lake was about two blocks long. We swam back and forth, sometimes twice, Candy always leaving me way behind. We would rest at one end, chat for a while, and go on.

I remember with pleasure the constant movement of arms and legs. Candy's swift and easy strokes. The sometimes conscious changing of the movement patterns, always trying to improve them, do them better, smoother. Just like everything else.

It was great to swim in that lake with Candy.

*

"1. *Devotion—Prayer* (Bhakti Yoga). This is probably the first spiritually oriented activity that people practice since most of us are taught to pray as children. If not, later in life, when, out of need and suffering, we turn to God for help, we may start talking and praying to that unseen spirit animating us.

"The Sanskrit word Bhakti means 'devotion.' So to practice this form of yoga is to express some kind of devotion, whether directly to God or indirectly through a particular Saint, Master, or Guru who spiritually inspires us. It could be directed to any of the Great Masters or to one of the lesser known saints or teachers that have lived, whether or not related to one of the great religions. Any kind of devotion sincerely expressed, no matter to whom, always ends up going to the Supreme Being.

"Devotion can be practiced in our homes, in a temple, synagogue, church, or wherever we happen to be. However, those of us who really understand and practice devotion have a small altar at home where we display the image or images of the object of our devotion, adorned with plants, flowers, small objects, etc.

"This activity yields better fruits when done in private, for then we feel more at ease to express ourselves and make the experience real. At least twice daily, preferably at the beginning and the end of the day, we should manifest our devotion before our altar in whatever words come from our heart.

"Devotion's most common form is prayer, and it can be expressed in an informal or a formal way.

"*Informal Prayer.* Informal, spontaneous prayer is probably the first direct contact human beings ever had with the Supreme Power they later called God.

"When man realized that a natural order exists around him, he also realized that there must be someone or something that was directing it all and that probably had created it all. This realization created the desire to communicate with that Supreme Power to find guidance and comfort.

"Informal prayer is just kneeling humbly and spontaneously saying to God whatever we feel, whatever comes out of our mouth. It is a most beautiful and direct contact with our loving and merciful Father. During those private moments we can really pour out our hearts and establish a very close relationship with our Divine Father.

"When we pray informally, we can start by thanking our Father for anything good or positive that we think about ourselves, past or present—for anything good that we have or that happens to us is only thanks to Him. Then we can express our gratitude for whatever good has been currently happening to us, and, eventually, as we reach higher levels of consciousness, we will even thank Him for events that seem negative as we realize that they only happen to help us grow.

"Afterwards we can express whatever we feel like expressing, whatever comes out, and, finally, we can ask for whatever we deeply feel like asking for. But these requests should be of a higher level, not selfish, small demands. The small things are always given to us; we do not have to ask for them. Be sure that whatever we ask for sincerely in prayer, we will receive.

"Yes, informal spontaneous prayer, this simple activity, will not only bring great relief from anxiety, but also, as we listen to our words, we will get to know ourselves better and gradually realize what we really want in life. It will definitely improve our general well-being and surely lead us into the wonderful realm of love.

"*Formal Prayer*. As man advanced and created higher forms of culture, the natural need for a relationship with God also developed, and different forms of worship and ritual came into existence. They were called religions, from the Latin word *religare*, which means 'to unite,' to unite with God. It was then that formal prayer began.

"As civilizations developed, some men, highly inspired by Divine Energy and experiencing great admiration and love for all of creation, started to express their feelings and gratitude in verse or prose, thus creating formal prayers, some of which have become very well known among the different religions.

"But some of these formal prayers were written or altered by the organizers of religion for the specific purpose of influencing people's minds and keeping them under their ascendancy. These do not convey high, pure feelings but some confusion and negativity instead.

"If we like one of these well-known prayers and feel inspired by it, it is wonderful to make it our own and say it as part of our devotional ritual. Yet, we should try to really understand, agree with it, convey what it says, and learn to enjoy it; we will surely receive its benefits. We can change some of its words if we feel like it.

"If, by chance or through research, we come across a lesser known piece by which we feel inspired, let's also make it our own and find the time to say it and enjoy it.

"We should learn prayers by heart and say them every day, not only for our pleasure, but because our whole being will gradually register their positive and divine message and improve itself in every sense. Praying is also a wonderful source of relief and support and another precious way to keep storing positive information in our brain-computer-minds. It will surely help improve our lives and bring us to experience moments of great joy. Perhaps one day we will find ourselves saying, 'Thank you, Father, thank you for so much care, so much love, so much well-being.' "

*

I already knew about prayer, and how! I certainly knew about the beauty and power of prayer. I always turned to prayer whenever I experienced difficult times, then developed the habit of practicing it twice daily. Prayer guided me to that direct and beautiful contact with God which marked the beginning of an evermore enjoyable and conscious life. Prayer has been my most important practice.

I want to share with you a wonderful piece from "The Sermon on the Mount" that I have practiced as a prayer, almost every day for many years, at my early evening ritual.

"I shouldn't give thought in my life for what I shall drink, or what I shall eat, or what I shall put on. Isn't life more important than food, and body than clothes?

"I observe the birds of the air and see that they sow not, neither do they reap, nor gather into barns. Yet you, Heavenly Father, feed them. Am I not much better than they?

"I observe the wild lilies and see that they toil not, neither do they spin, and yet, not even the greatest king, in all his glory, has ever been arrayed like one of them.

"And, Father, why give thought to clothes? I observe the grass of the field which today is so beautiful and tomorrow is cast into the oven. Why would you not clothe me much better? Oh, man of little faith that I am!

"So, Father, I shouldn't give thought in my life to what I shall drink, or to what I shall eat, or to what I shall put on; because you, Heavenly Father, know that I have need of all those things.

"First, my Lord, I shall search for your Kingdom and your righteousness, and all those things will be given unto me. I shall not give thought for the morrow, for the morrow will give thought to the things of itself. Let each day take care of its own chores."

Yes, I have certainly experienced the exquisite beauty and power of praying, and the ever growing love and well-being it has contributed to me. . . .

What a beautiful body Candy had. How good it looked in her black bikini. She had spent part of the afternoon with me at the park, swimming and practicing yoga near the ocean.

What a gift, what a pleasure to look at her, to be with her. To listen to whatever she had to say. Her big expressive eyes, her sense of humor.

But time flies. Back to work; "the voice" is waiting.

*

"2. *Reading—Studying* (Jnana Yoga). The word "*jnana*" means "to study" or "wisdom." This is the path of seeking union with God or knowing more about the spiritual dimension by means of reading and studying books on the subject. Whenever we read the *Bhagavad Gita*, the *Torah*, the *New Testament*, the *Koran*, or any other book of high spiritual content with the intention of trying to really understand it and acquire sound knowledge about the spiritual dimension, then we are practicing Jnana Yoga.

"Some people spend part of their lives trying to find spiritual knowledge in many different kinds of books. This, although often interesting, can be a waste of time. But why try to persuade anyone not to do it, since it is surely part of his or her process of evolution?

Yet, why not try to get to know more about the teachings of those who, throughout mankind's history, have been more successful as teachers of life, as spiritual leaders?

"Krishna, Moses, Buddha, Jesus, and Mohammed motivated many people, had many followers. Why do they still? There must be some very special reason. Thus, to do some studying about their lives and teachings seems like the right approach if one is interested in really learning about life and about the spiritual dimension.

"To practice Jnana Yoga, we must dedicate a daily amount of time to the study of a book with a high spiritual content. We should proceed slowly, letting it gradually unfold its wisdom. It is most recommended to do this reading aloud to ourselves; in such a way we have a better chance to grasp what it really conveys and make some of its truths our own."

*

After prayer, the next thing I did to try to find my way towards a better quality of life was to read books related to the spiritual dimension.

I would go to specialized bookstores and search, sometimes for hours, among many of these books. Then I would buy the ones that seemed the most interesting. Each book draws me gradually closer to the highest goal.

I would also talk to people that were on the same quest. From some of them I would hear about a particular book that, depending on my previous knowledge or intuition, I would buy or not. This is how I came upon The Great Initiates by Edward Schure, one of the most interesting and revealing books that I have ever read.

Reading books dedicated to the realm of the spirit is a very important activity if we want to learn about what the spiritual dimension offers. Not only for all the enjoyable and precious knowledge, but as we learn that so many different people, some of whom are very well-known, have talked or written about the same subject, we increasingly believe that there certainly must be some wonderful dimension or some wonderful experience that can be reached.

Now I have the habit of reading aloud to myself every day, sometimes only for a few minutes, short parts of a book conveying what I consider to be high spiritual knowledge. It is a great source of knowledge, support, and joy.

*

"3. *Chanting* (Japa Yoga). This is another beautiful activity that can help anyone get closer to God. We can chant alone or together with other people, in a formal or an informal way. Chanting or singing is one of the best known and oldest activities practiced by men in order to feel better, to reach higher, to experience love.

"From the time when men started living together, some kind of chanting or singing began to happen. It was surely one of the first means through which their souls drove them to express themselves. As the first spiritual rituals and religious ceremonies began to develop, some form of chanting was always an important part of them. Today it has become one of the most popular ways through which mankind seeks balance and expresses its feelings.

"As we hear different kinds of chants or songs, we will notice that some take us higher than others. And the more we learn and improve our education, the more we like the chanting or singing that conveys higher feelings. Eventually, perhaps, we will realize that certain chants and hymns sung in churches or temples are indeed very high, that we really enjoy them and that they make us feel especially good every time we hear them. Then we might decide to regularly attend one of these places in order to express our higher feelings and receive the high energy of others while chanting.

"Chanting can also be practiced individually. Some people practice it by themselves in their homes or places of worship.

"Yes, Japa Yoga or simply chanting is another way through which we can channel our Divine Energy which comes out of our souls and expresses itself in a beautiful way. Chanting is truly another precious activity that enables us to realize the existence of our soul, to become closer to God, and to experience real love."

＊

I still cherish my first significant experience with chanting. It was in Canada, near Toronto, in a beautiful boarding school close to a small town named Aurora.

I was placed there by my parents for high school and to learn English. We were supposed to attend church on Sundays and, as many of us know, most Protestant services have a lot of chanting. It was a new experience for me—in South America I had never done any singing during church services.

I still remember the small, beautiful chapel, all gray stone and dark wood. Beautiful and inspiring. I still remember how chanting there aroused in me deep and wonderful feelings. How chanting with others felt like a very good thing to do.

Back in South America, there was no more chanting and, not happy with what religion had to offer me there, I ceased to attend church and all activities related to it. Yet my intuition led me to maintain my relationship with Jesus and my constant search for the Truth, the only thing, I thought, that could bring real beauty and meaning to my life.

After several years I came in close contact with a religious group whose practices, derived from Hinduism, were basically various kinds of Yoga and again I experienced the joy of chanting songs of a high spiritual level. This brought me wonderful moments, feelings great and high.

Later on, more clear and relaxed about everything—Jesus having been my first and beloved source of inspiration—I felt like experiencing chanting in a familiar language and a Christian environment.

I searched for a while, attending a variety of Christian services, until one day I was captivated by an Episcopalian one. I liked it because there was a lot of chanting and because it had maintained, in a way easy to relate to, the well-organized ritual to celebrate and inspire a good relationship with God that I feel is necessary in a church. Then I realized that my cherished childhood church in Canada had been Episcopalian.

Thus, for years now, I have been chanting mainly at Episcopal and Hindu oriented services and always experiencing beautiful sweetness and true joy.

*

"4. *Body Postures* (Hatha Yoga). It is so important to stimulate the body through exercise that, since the beginning of civilization, men who reached higher levels of consciousness realized this fact and soon started to develop and practice it. Just the same, other men with even higher levels of consciousness, guided by divine inspiration, started to develop special movements and postures for the purpose of enhancing and maintaining all the functions and parts of the body in perfect shape. They learned that this practice would lead them ever closer to being one with God.

"Thus, the orderly sequence of body movements and postures performed in tune to the rhythm of our breath, is what today we call Hatha Yoga. It has been evolving through the centuries since very ancient times in order to properly enhance and maintain all the functions and parts of our body, and bring us ever closer to being our real selves, ever closer to following God's guidance.

"As we slowly stretch the different parts of our body and hold them stretched for a few minutes, all in tune to the rhythm of our breath, we are releasing most of the tension accumulated as a result of our daily activities; we are giving the body time to get properly energized and renewed, and we are strengthening our muscles.

"As we stimulate the spinal cord, we are balancing and releasing the tension from our nervous system. This benefits all our inner functions—circulatory, digestive, respiratory and glandular—and properly adjusts our alertness and reactions.

"We are also stimulating our arteries and veins, which further improves our circulatory system, the carrier of oxygen and nutrients to all the cells of our body and brain.

"As we stretch our muscles and hold them stretched for a few minutes, we help them improve and maintain their elasticity and strength due to the tension, and their youthfulness due to the proper oxygenation.

"After a Hatha Yoga session, any signs of stress we might have felt disappear, as our whole system feels balanced and in harmony, for this extraordinary activity releases mental and physical tension and liberates repressed energy. We also experience a distinct and wonderful sense of clarity, relaxation, and renewal.

"Anyone can enjoy the benefits of Hatha Yoga. This is an individual process that can be practiced at any period of our lives. We simply adjust to the possibilities and willingness of our body and mind and let this practice take us to an ever increasing feeling of well-being.

"Yes, we all have a great potential to develop, and Hatha Yoga will surely contribute to bringing our body and mind to their proper alignment, development, and harmonious functioning. We will become ever more balanced, beautiful, creative, youthful human beings. Our life will improve in every sense.

"When properly performed, Hatha Yoga should be an effective meditation in itself, for it must be done with as much concentration as possible on its movements, postures, and rhythm of the breath. Since concentration is meditation, properly doing Hatha Yoga is like doing other kinds of meditation. Most people who really learn to practice it like it so much for the immediate results and ever increasing well-being they experience, that they acquire the habit of doing it two or three times a week.

"Moreover, through this practice we will develop a special and positive relationship with our body and become much more aware of how it functions. Yes, Hatha Yoga certainly contributes to bringing health and youth, mental and physical."

*

Soon after I started to practice Hatha Yoga, I began to experience a new feeling of well-being. I had already practiced many sports and outdoor activities to keep in shape and feel good, but none had given me the overall well-being, freshness, and high feelings that Hatha Yoga did. Plus, it felt so appropriate for the body; its practice was such a natural activity for the body to do—so individual, relaxing, stimulating, strengthening, revealing.

Finally, I did the Yoga Teachers Training Course at the Sivananda Yoga Camp near Montreal, Canada—a demanding course and training which certainly tested my whole being in various ways. Considering all the benefits it brought me, I am very glad to have accomplished it.

Now I enjoy practicing Hatha Yoga almost every day, reaping the benefits of its highly positive results. Teaching it has also become a serious and significant activity which I very much enjoy and benefit from.

That morning I was feeling especially good. The night before, Adriana had come to pick me up, and we had gone to Key Biscayne to have dinner at a small restaurant right on the beach. I had driven the car while we both enjoyed the exhilarating rhythm of Prokofiev's classical symphony.

As we got there, the full moon was already visible, just coming up from the horizon, enormous. We had dinner watching this magnificent thing gently rise. Afterwards we walked for a while along the beach, towards the park, where there was no one else at the time.

The sky was clear, the moonlight strong. Not only the tranquil water, but also the leaves from the palm trees glowed with it. A night to remember.

I am usually waiting for the magic of the full moon to do something special.

*

"5. *Meditation* (Raja Yoga). Many people today practice meditation for different purposes. Some do it to overcome anguish or stress, some to control the mind, some to get high, some to raise their level of consciousness, others to establish a deep spiritual connection with the Supreme Being or Force. And, no doubt, meditation, which can be a beautiful and pleasant activity, can serve all these different purposes.

"Yet, since the dawn of civilization, some spiritual teachers have been teaching their disciples different methods of meditation. These techniques, they assure us, will gradually raise our level of consciousness and help bring us to enlightenment, in other words, bring us to be one with God's will and harmony, to experience real freedom, love, and well-being.

"But, among these different methods of meditation, some are better than others. The better they are, the more they help us concentrate and stop the relentless thinking process of the mind, thus allowing a higher process to take place.

"Some of these methods use the mind itself as a means of practice, as when we inwardly repeat a particular word or mantra. Some use one of the senses, especially the eyes, as when one concentrates upon a specific object such as a burning candle or a flower.

"Yet, the highest teachers say that neither the mind nor the senses should be used when practicing meditation. For one of the aims of the practice is precisely to quiet the mind and the senses so that the higher process can take place. Thus, the best techniques of meditation are those in which neither the mind nor the senses are used.

"Raja Yoga, literally translated as the 'King of Yogas,' is certainly the best, the highest, the most beautiful method of meditation. It consists of four specific meditation techniques discovered even before Hinduism was established as a religion, perhaps at the time of the almost mythical, great teacher Rama. Or maybe even before, perhaps at the beginning of the marvelous and remote civilizations of Egypt and Mesopotamia.

"In ancient times these four precious meditation techniques were revealed only to people who made great, long, and sincere efforts to learn them, people who would blindly obey their teacher for many years before they could learn even one of them. This probably was a way to test the sincerity and good intentions of the disciple and make sure he was worthy of knowing such very special practices. Or perhaps it was to test his endurance and make sure that he would persevere and practice the techniques once he learned them. Or maybe the hard requirements were to have the disciple realize that what he wanted to learn was indeed very precious. In any case, these techniques were not revealed to people unless they became fully aware of their purpose and eager to practice them.

"Over the centuries, some teachers became less strict about revealing these techniques to their disciples. Buddha taught them to a good number of people who did not have to wait too long to learn them. Jesus probably taught them to people only a few months, sometimes maybe even weeks, after becoming his disciples.

"Today, all or some of these techniques are being taught by gurus or teachers all over the world. Yet each one of these teachers has a different level of consciousness or degree of 'highness,' and a different way of teaching. Thus, it makes a great difference from whom we receive this very precious knowledge.

"The practice of Raja Yoga should be learned from a guru or teacher with a high level of consciousness, who has thoroughly mastered the techniques and knows how to properly reveal them.

"Sometimes the names of the techniques are mentioned in famous spiritual works, such as the *Bhagavad Gita*, the *Bible*, the *Tao Te Ching*, the *Teachings of Buddha*, the *Koran*, etc., but without explaining what they really mean. Thus, very few people are aware of what these names really express.

"Raja Yoga should be learned with absolute honesty, otherwise it will not work. It cannot be bought for any amount of money, and no real spiritual guru will sell it. If money is involved, it will not work.

"Moreover, these techniques will only be effective for a disciple who receives them from a guru or teacher with a high level of consciousness, and by following the guru's conditions and ways of doing things. The aspirant or disciple should be patient and sincere, for only when received under the right flow of circumstances will this knowledge yield its marvelous fruits.

"Nevertheless, one of these techniques will be fully described and explained here for the following reasons: first, because this technique has already been mentioned in some books and it is practiced, often erroneously, by many people who ignore its full significance and purpose. Second, because it will help many others gain the very important realization that the essence and source of the teachings of the Great Masters has always been the same. Third, due to the confusing and troublesome state the world is in today, it would be very positive if many other people learn about it or understand it better, and perhaps feel inspired to practice it and experience its benefits, thus improving their lives and the world around them.

"The techniques through which we can get in direct contact with our soul—our energy within, that part of God that dwells inside of us—and receive the highest benefits, are: The Holy Breath, the Light, the Music and the Nectar.

"*The Holy Breath, Holy Name, Holy Spirit, or Holy Word.* Often mentioned in the *Bhagavad Gita* as the 'Atman,' by Moses and Jesus in the *Bible,* by Buddha as 'meditation of the heart,' and by Mohammed as 'The Spirit of God'—this meditation technique is surely one of the most positive activities a human being can ever do.

"The term 'Holy Breath' and its synonyms simply mean that through our breath, especially deep conscious breathing, we are in direct contact with our Divine Father Supreme Being. In other words, our soul is in permanent contact with God through our breath, but especially when we consciously sit down and dedicate some time just to feel and experience our breathing process.

"Let us not be fooled by the simplicity of this activity. Its very simplicity has fooled many others before. The very fact that the Great Masters had so many faithful—and even fanatical—followers is most significant. The Masters were teaching something highly meaningful, something that truly improved people's lives, something that could be experienced directly. Thus, let us not be fooled by its simplicity; this is the highest knowledge a person can learn, and the only way to confirm it is to practice it and experience the results.

"Therefore, let us set aside some time, preferably early in the morning after some moments of purifying prayer and maybe a few yoga postures, to sit down in a cross-legged or comfortable, upright position and just experience our breath: gently concentrating on it, in and out, up and down, deeply, easily, gently . . . just letting go and simply experiencing that beautiful source of energy, harmony, knowledge, love, and peace.

"Let us remain there for a while, as long as we feel like it, as long as it feels right. Maybe fifteen minutes, or thirty, maybe more. It is such a beautiful thing to do and can feel so good, that surely those who try it with humility will experience immediate benefits and easily acquire the habit of doing it daily.

"Even better, if we also practice in the early evening, as we get home from work, perhaps after or before a few stretches or yoga

postures, concentrating on our breath will certainly bring wonderful relaxation and help process correctly all events and thoughts
experienced that day; and, of course, it will renew our whole being
to properly enjoy the evening.

"These precious meditation techniques can be done formally,
as when we sit down just to practice, or informally, whenever we
remember, any time during the day, as when we walk or drive. We
will immediately feel centered and relaxed.

"We should not practice this meditation expecting any results;
no selfish motivation should be involved. Our only aim as we sit
is to be with the Holy Breath, to go within and experience the
soothing movement and sound caused by our breathing process.
Yet we will always experience some benefits, especially when we
practice formally, sitting down and dedicating a specific amount
of time to it.

"This is the Holy Breath, the Holy Spirit mentioned so many
times in the New Testament. This is the main source from which
all the Great Masters and many other outstanding men, such as
Ghandi, have drawn their knowledge, endurance, strength, and
love.

"This, perhaps, is the main practice that will gradually lead us
to feel better and happier, to higher levels of consciousness, harmony, love, and strength, to really enjoy life and truly understand
its meaning, to really get to be our own pure selves.

"But this practice should not be done too much or too intensely, for only its natural process, which cannot be forced, will
bless us with its benefits. Let us do it gently, enjoy it, and, day by
day, patiently feel grateful for whatever benefits we experience."

*

The Holy Breath. The unique pleasure of being with the Holy Breath
. . . no words can describe it.

I have long been familiar with it, and I am doing my best to be with it more often. It has greatly improved my life and given me many beautiful, memorable moments. Life has become ever more real, giving, and exciting thanks to it.

Yes, The Holy Breath, the beauty of its practice, and its marvelous rewards. . . . I wish I could describe it better, but, like anything else, to really know something one has to experience it.

I recommend using ear plugs when practicing this meditation technique. Thus, one can feel one's breathing process much better and more strongly, and concentration becomes easier. Remember to bring the tongue up and backwards and place it up along the palate; this will enhance the practice.

I breathed deeply, feeling grateful. Bucky turned his head up and looked at me. He wanted me to take him out, but I felt like working a little more—I really enjoyed what I was writing.

*

"LET US MENTION THE OTHER THREE meditation techniques that form part of this highest method. How to do them will not be explained because their practice should only be learned through personal instruction from a qualified teacher.

"*The Light.* When we practice this technique, we may see a beautiful, bright light in the shape of a thick circle. This light, caused by the Divine Energy that dwells inside of us, not only makes us feel immensely blessed and high, but also strongly supports our effort towards reaching enlightenment and freedom.

"When Jesus said, 'Many prophets and kings wished to see the things that you see, and did not see them,' he was referring particularly to this light.

"*The Music.* When we perform this technique we may hear a constant, harmonious, relaxing, and soothing sound or music also caused by the Divine Energy we have inside. This inner music, apart from bringing us comfort and relaxation, helps us become more balanced, harmonious, and in tune with ourselves and the world around.

"When Jesus said, 'Many prophets and kings wished to hear the things that you hear, and did not hear them,' he was referring to this sound or music.

"The Nectar. Those who practice this very special technique will sometimes taste a precious nectar, a sort of sweet substance, also produced by that Divine Energy we all have inside. This nectar will make us feel particularly good and high, and definitely support our gradual path towards the highest experience of living in union with God. Many references to this technique can be read in the *Bible* and other books of high spiritual content.

"If anyone is interested in learning the practice of these three other techniques, a teacher or guru with a high level of consciousness must be found to learn them from."

*

Now it is appropriate to quote some of the words of the Great Masters concerning Raja Yoga.

> On this earth there is no purifier
> As great as this Knowledge.
> When a man is made perfect with Yoga,
> He knows the truth within his heart.
> Krishna, *Bhagavad Gita*

> A yogi should retire into a solitary place,
> Exercise control over body and mind,
> And unceasingly meditate on the Atman.
> Krishna, *Bhagavad Gita*

The secret things belong to the Lord, our God.
But the things revealed
Belong to us and our sons forever.

Moses, Deuteronomy 29

Josua was filled with the Spirit of Wisdom
For Moses had laid his hands on him.

Moses, Deuteronomy 34

By methods of concentration and meditation
One can subdue the self and achieve Nirvana.

Buddha, Doctrine of the Buddha

It is only when a man,
Ceasing to attend to any outward thing,
Becomes plunged in that devout meditation of heart
When he can be at ease and reach the highest.

Buddha, Doctrine of the Buddha

There is a silence where the soul may meet God,
And there the source of wisdom is,
And all who enter are immersed in light,
And filled with love and rightful power.

Jesus, Aquarian Gospel 40

That which is born of flesh is child of man,
That which is born of Holy Breath is child of God.

Jesus, Aquarian Gospel 75

Many prophets and kings
Wished to see the things which you see
And did not see them;
Wished to hear the things that you hear
And did not hear them.

Jesus, Luke 10

Unless one is born of water and the Spirit,
One cannot enter the Kingdom of God.

Jesus, John 3

John baptized with water,
But you shall be baptized with the Holy Spirit
Not many days from now.

Jesus, Acts 1

Your Lord said to the angels:
I am creating man from clay;
When I have fashioned him
And breathed of my Spirit into him, kneel down,
And prostrate yourselves before him.

Mohammed, Koran 8

*

Those beautiful quotations. That precious information. It is difficult to describe what I sometimes felt as I finished working with "the voice" in some of the sessions of this book. It was sort of a gentle, overwhelming feeling of awe and humility.

That afternoon, as I was biking to the park, I was learning by heart part 5 of "Song of Myself," that magnificent poem by Walt Whitman . . . just repeating it time after time, trying to get meaning and sound memory.

As I continuously repeated the second part, particularly the phrase "And that all the men ever born are also my brothers," I felt a very deep and strong emotion and, all of a sudden, abundant tears started to flow out of my eyes, an outburst of tears such as I had never experienced before. Then a great relief, as if some enormous weight had just fallen from me.

I realized that all the men that have ever existed and that exist today are really brothers that come from the same source. Then I understood the Greeks and the Romans and all the rest, present and past, like I had never understood them before.

That afternoon I lost most of the irrational distrust and fear of people that I had been carrying with me for so long. It was like shedding a great deal of weight, of Karma. Since then, I have felt much better among others, and I am increasingly learning to enjoy their company.

*

"6. *Service* (Karma Yoga). The word 'karma' can be interpreted in different ways, conveying different meanings; one of them is 'to serve.'

"According to this meaning, Karma Yoga can be considered as disinterested action or service performed to benefit the world. These actions should not be done with the intention of obtaining any kind of gain whatsoever.

"In other words, union with God through Karma Yoga happens when we give our time to perform some kind of service for any other person or persons or institution without any ulterior motivation such as material remuneration or social advantage. Our sole motivation must be the natural urge to help others in order to grow spiritually, to get closer to God. This attitude, though, is not the highest.

"The highest form of Karma Yoga occurs when we serve others purely motivated by love, pure disinterested love and care for the world around us, love for humanity, love for God's creation."

*

Suddenly "the voice" stopped. Then I decided to explain, myself, another conception of the word "karma."

According to some Hindu theories, we are all born, or come into the world, with a certain amount of debt or "karma" to pay. Karma, here, means a negative balance accumulated through negative actions performed in past lives due to our imperfection. Thus, every time our soul is given a human body, it is just another chance to pay some of its karma or debt and so become closer to God's will and perfection.

In other words, this life is another opportunity given us to become closer to perfection, to God. If we take proper advantage of it and pay our karma, we will not be reborn again in this world but, instead, become part of the infinite perfection of God.

Thus, if souls reincarnate in human bodies and come into this world for as long as they have some karma to pay, then everyone that now lives on this earth is not yet "one with God," but simply having the chance to get closer to Him.

As it is difficult to support the theory of reincarnation, it is easier to believe that each one of us is just part of the great process of evolution taking place in the universe, our particular human process happening on planet earth—a process of evolution towards perfection, harmony, union with God.

It is obvious that, considering man's long history on this planet, we have evolved, though slowly, for the better. And we will reach the peak as a group when most people on earth enjoy real respect, freedom, and well-being.

As individuals, we reach the peak when we attain levels of consciousness high enough that we can live in creative harmony with our planet and other fellow humans according to the transcendental laws of nature—in other words, when we reach harmony, union with God.

All things, including human beings, are at different levels of evolution, some closer to perfection than others. This is what makes the difference between a beautiful diamond and a rough carbon, between a gentle, honest, happy person, close to God and a violent, dishonest, miserable person far from the natural will of the Creator.

Why are some people born with a higher level of evolution, mentally and physically, than others? It is probably natural selec-tion. Obviously, we inherit through our genes, more or less, the level of evolution our parents had, our grandparents had, and so on. But certainly there is something else going on, and we surely have the opportunity of gradually evolving and improving our own level, and thus our genes, during this lifetime on earth.

There is also a third, interesting, and significant meaning to the word "karma," which is the positive or negative balance that we create for ourselves through our actions.

In this context, every action we perform, no matter how unimportant it may seem, creates a reaction. Sometimes immedi-ately, sometimes within days, sometimes later. But it always does.

Positive actions bring positive reactions. Negative actions bring negative reactions. In other words, positive actions create good karma, while negative actions create bad karma.

In this sense, karma is the positivity or negativity that we bring to ourselves by our actions.

What has Karma Yoga or Service done for me? What has the experience of selfless service given to my life? It is hard to put it into words, but I am going to try.

First of all, it clearly showed me my own selfishness and how difficult it is to really give selflessly—especially in a period of my life when I thought I needed most of my time to dedicate to what I considered my most important activities.

This happened when, a little depressed, I moved to live for a while at a Yoga Center. There it was firmly suggested to the residents to do a few hours of Karma Yoga every week. I did it, and, to my surprise, I immediately started to feel better, understand life better, and everything I did improved.

Among regular household chores, every week I gave a Hatha Yoga class and also cooked dinner for a group of about two to three dozen people. In both activities, I certainly gave a definite amount of time and offered valuable knowledge acquired through years of practice. By doing these things, I gained a much better sense of really *giving* a valuable part of myself and life—very different from the feeling I got when I wrote a check or gave money.

Furthermore, it gave me the feeling of being a good person and a new sense of understanding the necessities of others and caring for them; the knowledge that to *receive* from life or people, and really appreciate it, one has to learn to give selflessly, from one's heart. It also increased my self-esteem, that feeling of being a more significant and lovable person.

Perhaps most important, it has led me to learn more about love, to really give out of love, to better recognize love in myself and others, to further experience the wonderful feeling of real love.

I guess I can also say that selfless service definitely helps me feel more worthy of occupying a space on this planet and truly enjoying what it has to offer.

*

"7. *Proper Sleep*. This, again, is one of the most important aspects of human life. Not only for what has been already mentioned in the preceding chapters relating to the body and the mind, but because it is mostly at night, when we sleep, that our Heavenly Father Universal Energy carefully works on us and gradually brings us to higher levels of harmony, knowledge, and love.

"Yes, it is mostly at night during sleep that the Divine Energy subtly works on us, through our soul, over our whole system, and somehow makes it work better, improves it, makes it behave more and more in tune to natural harmony, to what is naturally right and beautiful.

"This is why, when we start a new day, sometimes we find ourselves doing things and responding to things much better than we did before. This is why oftentimes, in a new day, we discover ourselves understanding life and our relationships with others more clearly and feeling more compassion and love for the world around us.

"This positive process of evolution while sleeping should happen to everybody to a certain extent, but this varies. It happens in higher degrees depending on how much our body and brain are free from toxicity, on how much our brain-mind is at peace, pure and open to this subtle touch. It happens much more to those who regularly practice activities to keep in constant touch with their soul, and through it establish a stronger contact with the Universal Energy God, making themselves more receptive to this magic touch. It happens a little, or not at all, to those who live mostly to please their senses and to keep their bodies and brains intoxicated, their energy wasted.

"It is definitely important to properly prepare ourselves each evening to have a good night's sleep, so that our Heavenly Father can work upon us and gradually make better and happier human beings out of us."

*

This interesting and revealing passage made me ponder and realize that lately I may have been noticing—I am almost sure—that some kind of important process is happening to me at night.

Thus, it seems right to quote some words said by Jesus and written in *The Essene Gospel of Peace*, that confirm such a process.

"But when the sun is set, and your Heavenly Father sends you his most precious angel, sleep, take your rest and be all night with the angel of sleep. Then your Heavenly Father will send you his unknown angels, that they may be with you the livelong night. And the Heavenly Father's unknown angels will teach you many things concerning the Kingdom of God, even as the angels of the Earthly Mother, instruct you in the things of her kingdom.

"I tell you truly, you will be every night the guests in the kingdom of your Heavenly Father, if you do his commandments. And when you wake up upon the morrow, you will feel in you the power of the unknown angels. And your Heavenly Father will send them to you every night, that they may build your spirit, even as every day the Earthly Mother sends you her angels, that they may build your body."

This passage certainly refers to a very important part of our lives that very few of us are aware of—shall we say the "magic" part of our lives? Yet, once we are consciously on the "path," many things seem like magic.

That morning I had started working very early, so it was time to stop, eat something, and go renew myself at the divine magic park near the ocean.

*

"8. *Contact with Nature*. This is a most beautiful and pleasant way to be in close contact with God's Divine Energy. Though this Energy is everywhere, it is especially pure and strong in every manifestation of nature.

"Flowers, plants, trees, fields, streams, mountains, rivers, oceans, clouds, sun, moon, stars, and many other forms of nature are all one with God, full of Divine Energy. Whenever we are in close contact with any of these, we are receiving God's pure, healing, enlightening, and strong energy.

"We should acquire the habit of regularly practicing one or more outdoor activities—activities that take us out of the city and into close contact with nature. No doubt, we will notice that every time we do it, we will come back feeling better, lighter, and with a clearer vision about ourselves and life.

"Hiking is especially recommended—a refreshing activity, easy to perform at almost any age and condition, that not only can be a wonderful exercise and stimulus for the whole body, but that also brings us closer to God than most other outdoor experiences, for it is performed at a pace in harmony to our nature. We will especially benefit from it if we enter deep into woods or fields or along the seashore, far away from any disturbing manifestations of society, such as roads, buildings, cars, motorcycles, etc.

"Contact with nature will certainly help bring us closer to balance, harmony, and well-being."

*

I will always remember one pleasant sunny afternoon when, with a dear cousin, we hiked up part of the mountain under which Caracas stands. How later, while the sun was setting, we peacefully sat under tall, brilliant, and dancing eucalyptus trees and talked and looked at the splendid scenery around and below us. How she told me that lately she had been doing some nature travels and hikes with a particular group of people and how, since then, her understanding of life and her approach to it had significantly changed for the better. "I became another person," she said.

*

"9. *Proper Sexual Behavior*. Though secondary, this is a very important aspect of our lives. A very important aspect that, due to its strong presence and consequences, depending on how we approach it, can certainly affect everything else in our lives in a positive or a negative way.

"Every time we have a sexual relationship, our whole being gets involved. Our bodies play a definite role. Our minds can also be substantially implicated. Our souls, the most sensitive part of our beings, are there all the way, holding out or giving in.

"Yet the big difference lies in whether the relationship was motivated by the soul or was provoked by the mind. Because, no doubt, concerning sex, our bodies are ultimately under the command of either our minds or our souls.

"If a relationship occurs with the acceptance or motivation of our souls, there will not be negative results. But if it is instigated by our minds, in disharmony and restlessness, then we will suffer negative consequences; there will be a price to pay.

"In other words, when relationships occur naturally with people we respect and love, they will become a positive part of our living process, and we will fully enjoy the pleasure that comes with it. But when they happen, provoked by one of the many reasons our minds can think of, with somebody we do not really like or love, then we will not obtain full pleasure from it, and we will suffer negative results.

"Moreover, when we perform a sexual act, by ourselves or with someone else, a great amount of energy goes with it. A great amount of precious energy that, unless spent having a wonderful experience, should be employed doing other activities that bring positive fruits. There usually is too much energy spent in mediocre or negative sexual relationships.

"It must be clearly understood that sexual relationships were given by God-Nature to animals and men for the purpose of procreation, evolution. Since the main purpose of human life is to reach the highest possible level of consciousness and become as close as possible to God's harmony, procreation is not the most important part of a human being's life.

"When many more people become aware of the chance to reach the highest and most beautiful prize and let such a path become part of their lives, less and less sex will happen in the world. Then most of mankind will gradually get closer to living in balance and harmony with the environment and creating a state of paradise here on earth.

"As for homosexual relationships, though not as common as heterosexual ones, most are primarily urged by the mind to fulfill the deep vacuum that comes from not experiencing real love. These relationships can also be part of a human being's conscious process of evolution and an experience through which people may evolve towards the highest goal.

"People that perform homosexual acts deserve the same respect we give to others. They are also God's creatures. Many carry this drive in their genes. Others acquired it by growing up under negative circumstances or in reaction to life experiences. Nevertheless, most suffer a great deal due to the negative approach that so many others today have towards homosexuality.

"It is not right to despise or disrespect the doings of nature, even if they seem abnormal, but to accept the hand of God and help those who suffer. This would be exactly what a man of God, like Jesus, would do.

"The crucial point is not with whom we have sex, but to really like, love, and respect the person with whom we are going to have sex: not to become a slave of our sexual drive, not to be unconsciously promiscuous but, like true human beings, to have sex only when it is in harmony with the guidance of our souls. The more we experience real love in our lives, the less we feel like having sex other than that accepted by our souls.

"It is important to realize that sex plays a secondary role in our life process—that our sexual behavior, like everything else, will evolve positively as we reach higher levels of consciousness and well-being.

"The human body is a beautiful part of creation that can be much admired and enjoyed. Its beauty mainly depends on the care and love we give it. The body's main purpose is to help us reach the highest goal, thus it is very worthy of our care, love, and respect. Consider it as such, and let us love and respect our bodies as well as the bodies of others. Let us learn to rightfully admire and properly enjoy that beautiful part of God."

*

It was good to learn "the voice's" message about sex. It has been helping me to cope much better with it.

To me, sex has always been a difficult thing to understand and deal with, a difficult thing to control and give its proper place.

I have seen so many people suffering with problems caused by their sexual behavior, so many people suffering due to the inhuman and negative approach that some of the great religions have towards sex.

What about the enormous tragedy and suffering caused by over-population? And yet, most religious leaders seem to ignore it. Is not over-population the result of improper sexual behavior due to the fact that so many people have a lower level of consciousness?

It is interesting to point out that for thousands of years, before the advent of Christian religious concepts, most of which were not set up by Jesus, bisexuality was a normal way of life among most civilizations.

I just sat for a while, looking around, trying to find more words to express my feelings about sex. Then I looked up to the sky, beautiful and blue, and hoped for the best.

*

TO CLOSE THIS CHAPTER ABOUT THE SOUL, it is appropriate to confirm that these different kinds of activities are the highest spiritually oriented activities that can be practiced. Through patient and sincere daily practice we can surely overcome, over the years, any amount of confusion, imbalance or 'karma' that we may carry, to eventually become real and happy human beings.

"Once we start practicing, we will enter a daily, conscious, evolutionary process that will fill our lives with adventure, meaning, and wonderful rewards. But especially, it will take us to experience the highest joy of love—the highest joy of really loving others and being loved by those who have also learned to love."

*

Suddenly I realized that "the voice's" message was over, that "our work" together was over. It took me by surprise, I had become accustomed to the pleasure of sitting down quietly, with humility, to just listen and write precious knowledge, beautiful words.

It had been several months, and now it seemed such a short time. Once again I felt deep emotion, gratitude, and bliss.

The blazing fire turns wood to ashes.
The fire of Knowledge turns all karmas to ashes.

Krishna, *Bhagavad Gita*

The highest state of being,
Can only be achieved through devotion to Him,
In whom all creatures exist,
By whom this universe is pervaded.

Krishna, *Bhagavad Gita*

Turn to the Lord your God
With all your heart and with all your soul.
This commandment is not difficult for you,
Nor is it out of reach,
For the Word is very near you,
In your mouth and in your heart,
That you may observe it.

Moses, *Deuteronomy 29*

Our soul is oppressed
When our thoughts and actions
Are not coming from it.

Buddha, *Doctrine of the Buddha*

All birth leads to suffering and death,
Unless the path to escape,
The way to enter into Nirvana,
Is found.

Buddha, *Doctrine of the Buddha*

The doctrine and the discipline
Which I have taught and preached
Will be your master after my death.

Buddha, *Doctrine of the Buddha*

But you, when you pray,
Go into your inner room,
And when you have shut your door,
Pray to your Father who can hear you;
And your Father will repay you.

> Jesus, *Matthew* 6

And all things you ask in prayer,
Believing,
You shall receive.

> Jesus, *Matthew* 21

God sings for us
Through bird and harpsichord and human voice.

> Jesus, *Aquarian Gospel* 12

To be subject to our God of Love,
Give your life and all you have
In willing service to the sons of men.

> Jesus, *Aquarian Gospel* 29

By the heaven and Him that built it;
By the earth and Him that spread it;
By the soul and Him that molded it
And inspired it with knowledge of sin and piety.

> Mohammed, *Koran* 91

One God,
Many Religions

A few days after I finished writing "the voice's" message, I started to improve the writing style and to edit. My English certainly required correcting.

Soon, I persistently began to feel that I wanted to say something else. When I clearly knew what it was and felt sure about doing it, I sat down once more to write an additional chapter.

But I did not start early the next morning. The night before Robert's parents had come for dinner. He wanted to make a good impression, so we thoroughly cleaned the house, set everything in order, and bought flowers. I did my best to create a tasteful, good-looking, well-balanced, vegetarian dinner.

They were not vegetarian, far from it, but Robert wanted to show them they could eat very well without animal products. I made, with Candy's help, a dish of brown rice with mushrooms and parsley, another one of stir-fried well-selected vegetables, some chick-peas with onions and bits of kale, and an avocado, watercress and lettuce salad with sunflower seed dressing. For dessert we had a delicious whole-wheat, sugarless pecan pie from a good vegetarian restaurant.

Robert's parents had a good time. They are well-educated people with good manners, conservative but open. And yes, manners and nice ways of doing things are important. Some people make fun of them or call them mannerisms. But refined behavior, especially at the dinner table, is something that comes naturally as our level of consciousness becomes higher.

In other words, good manners or cultivated ways of behavior have not been made up by the complicated minds of a very few. On the contrary, they have developed naturally in every important civilization as some men, reaching higher levels of consciousness and education, gradually learned to appreciate the orderly simplicity of life.

Doing things with gentleness and simplicity certainly makes a big difference. It is such a pleasure to relate to people who manifest themselves with gentleness and simplicity, who do not hurt our senses or feelings.

Anyway, it was a pleasant evening, and the three of us, after doing the dishes, decided to go swimming in the nearby lake. The night was warm and clear.

As I looked at my friends swimming away, gradually disappearing in the darkness, I remembered the famous phrase of many wise men, "It is much more difficult to master the art of living than any other expression of art."

*

1. About "The Highest Knowledge." As already stated, what was written in the four preceding chapters expressing "the voice's" message is basically the knowledge that the Great Masters were teaching their followers to practice, so that they could attain more union with God's harmony and, as a result, significantly improve their lives. Some teachers gave more emphasis to a particular aspect of the practice depending on the teacher's own experience and evolution.

It is well-known that most Eastern religions give great importance to the care of the body. Yet, though one can read in the

Essene Gospels the extensive instructions that Jesus gave his followers concerning the care of the body, it is surprising that the *New Testament* mentions so little about it. Nevertheless, any person with common sense soon realizes that we must take good care of our bodies in order to do and feel better. But, are there many of us with real common sense?

In any case, the way of eating recommended here is basically the same advised by the great sages throughout mankind's evolution on earth. Yet, one must bear in mind that they lived under different climates and that not all the products available to us were available to them. It is a matter of adapting the basic and natural principles of eating to our own circumstances.

All the great teachers have constantly spoken about the often negative influence to the mind on the facts of daily life and the outside world. They have given primordial importance to having the mind in harmony, for on this depends how close to God's guidance a man can get. And partly for this purpose, they have created and developed through the centuries the practice of the various spiritual activities already mentioned.

It was very appropriate to dedicate one chapter to the mind. First, because we all should be aware that we are not our mind, that our mind is just another part of our whole self. Then, because it is necessary to clearly understand the functioning and purpose of the mind to properly relate it to the circumstances and concepts of today's world.

When we have experienced various spiritual activities and have studied the essence of the most important religions, it becomes obvious that all the Great Masters have been teaching basically the same thing and have been closely related in their knowledge.

When we consider some of the Christian religions that sprang from the teachings of Jesus, we can see that they teach Bhakti Yoga when they talk about devotion or prayer. They also advise the practice of Jnana Yoga when they recommend reading the *Bible*. We realize that in many of their services, Japa Yoga is practiced when hymns are sung. We can also equate the practice of charity or service to Karma Yoga.

As for Raja Yoga or the highest form of meditation, Christians seldom mention it. Perhaps at the beginning, when organizing the first church, those in charge decided not to reveal the "top" secret to the majority. For then anybody could become "enlightened" and certainly disagree with some of the control, dogmas, and laws that the church considered convenient to establish and impose. Thereafter, in somewhat impure hands, that precious knowledge disappeared.

It could also be that those first organizers of the Church did not even learn about Raja Yoga since centuries earlier there had been a separation from Jesus's purest disciples. This seems more probable, for truly "enlightened" men would never have set up a church that would want to exercise so much material, political, and spiritual control over its followers.

To those familiar with Raja Yoga, or the highest form of meditation, it is obvious that when Jesus says, "And you shall be baptized with the Holy Spirit," he implies that it will be revealed to the disciples how to come into direct contact with their soul, God within, through the first meditation technique or Holy Breath. Finally, what Jesus really meant when he said, "Man shall not live on bread alone, but on every word that proceeds out of the mouth of God," was a reference to that regular breathing contact with the Holy Spirit or Holy Breath constantly reaching us.

Not everything the Masters have said has been recorded in the writings of their disciples or followers, nor has every word attributed to them been said by them. We must realize that most of these writings were written many years after the Master's death. Often based upon the word of usually uneducated disciples—frequently turned fanatics—many words and facts concerning their master's teachings and deeds have been misinterpreted or exaggerated. Yet, the knowledge offered in this book attempts to condense the essence of the Highest Truth, the basic knowledge that the Great Masters have been teaching.

*

I felt so good, I certainly felt better and better, increasingly learning to enjoy everything about life.

That afternoon at the park I read part of a fascinating article in *National Geographic* about the ancient temple of Borobudur in Indonesia. I cherished that magazine so much; it had, years ago, already become a very important part of my life. Its highly conscious and well written articles are not only a great source of news about what is going on in the world from a different and objective point of view, but also a constant source of deep feelings and high values.

I usually read all the titles and subtitles and the captions of all the photographs and charts or maps on each article every month. Then, I carefully read the articles that particularly interest me. I always read aloud to myself; this way I have a better chance to learn something about varied aspects of life and more about those especially attractive to me.

This simple, almost daily activity takes me about thirty minutes and has greatly improved my English and my general knowledge and understanding of the world. It has definitely been an exciting and highly positive entertainment.

The ocean was so beautiful, so clear, the tide especially low. A good number of people were walking far out, the water only up to around their knees or waist . . . a divine white egret was standing still nearby.

*

2. *One God, Many Religions.* When one studies and understands the main concepts and teachings of the great religions, it becomes obvious from their similarities that they come from the

same source of inspiration: God Divine Energy. Even if these concepts were not so similar, it is obvious that there cannot be a Supreme God for each different part of the world.

Thus, we must realize and accept that there is only one God, one Truth, and many religions. No religion has the exclusivity of God or Truth, for all were created by men inspired by the same and only God, just to help others fulfill the strong spiritual needs we all have.

We must realize that all religions are directed by human beings and none of us is perfect. Therefore, they are not always well directed and many mistakes are committed. Sometimes we can experience the blessing of finding a swami, a rabbi, a monk, or a priest with a high level of consciousness and love, but this is rare.

Thus, for our own good and regardless of circumstances, we must develop a private and personal relationship with that harmonizing being or force that we call God. Thereafter, we can enjoy the benefits and rituals of one or more religions, accepting what sincerely feels right and rejecting what does not.

When a religious leader insists on proclaiming the exclusivity or superiority of his religion, or on teaching confusing dogmas or rituals, he is not coming from God but from his own confused mind. These kinds of men are not very helpful; on the contrary, they are creating negativity, separating man from man, brother from brother, creating confusion and hatred.

Only when most of humanity realizes that there is only one God and many religions, then mankind will get on its way to evolving towards higher levels of well-being.

3. *All Religions are Sustained by Us*. We all have a strong natural need to somehow give spiritual nourishment to that part of God that dwells inside of us. Besides, it is the only way to attain peace of mind, feel good, and successfully go through life. As we try to fulfill this imperative need, most of us attend a church or a temple or some kind of congregation or other, thus sustaining such organizations with our attendance.

As many of us know, for most, the only way to get ever closer to God's harmony and well-being is by consciously practicing various spiritually oriented activities. As this requires some effort, especially at the beginning, it is usually easier to perform these practices in the company of other people as a source of inspiration and support. The main reason religions came to exist, created by men, is to offer all of us a favorable environment to worship and practice. As already mentioned, the word "religion" comes from the Latin word *religare*, which means "to unite, to bind together . . . to unite with God."

It can be wonderful to be part of a religious group that is really helping us become better and happier human beings, but, when this is not the case, we must find another way to better satisfy such an important need through another group or organization, or whatever feels right.

If we are really honest with ourselves, we know what feels right. Thus, to fulfill the imperative of spiritual nourishment or when looking for the right place to fulfill this necessity, most human beings, at some point, attend some kind of church or temple or group, usually getting something positive out of it. Yet, to be really successful, we must realize that this is an individual process. We can only reach higher levels of consciousness and well-being by sincere conscious practice in our homes, by our own individual effort, not by blindly attending a temple, synagogue, church, or mosque.

Therefore, we must have respect and tolerance for other people's individual process. We should accept and respect that each person or group of persons may have a different way of approaching worship or a different way of getting closer to God's harmony; it all depends on their level of consciousness. We should realize that most people do their best to fulfill their spiritual needs, and they can only follow their own process.

We are all brothers and sisters created by one God and living under the same roof. We are not feeling and understanding God's will and love when we do not accept, love, and respect all of creation, beginning with ourselves. Those who do not accept and tolerate other people's religions or ways of worship are not with God.

Thus, to get closer to God's wonderful well-being is ultimately an individual effort; we do not depend on any religion to achieve that. Yet, all religions depend on us.

*

One night, before going to bed, I went out to see the sky; it was clear, full of stars. So the next morning I got up at four-thirty and, in Robert's car, drove to Key Biscayne to watch the sunrise.

In the windless, quiet space I walked towards the middle of the beach and placed a towel on the sand near the water, sat in cross-legged position, facing the ocean, and concentrated on my breath.

Each new breath made me feel better—ever more love and peace and joy. I felt very grateful for all the love and all the protection and all the beauty that my Father was letting me experience.

Opening my eyes now and then, I waited and waited as the sky turned clearer—consciously breathing, sometimes looking, enchanted by the ever changing purples, pinks, violets. Just breathing and looking at those spellbinding colors, absorbing them all deep into my being. Intensely waiting for the ultimate priceless gift.

Each new breath brought more joy, peace, well-being. I breathed deeply, fully, trying to fill my entire being with all the best my Father would give me. Deeply, fully. . . .

Finally, the great ball of fire started to appear, gently, slowly emerging from the water, so exciting, so generous, so powerful. Amazing vision, magical performance of nature, miracle. I remained there, fixed, until all the magnificent vision was up in the air.

I walked back to the car feeling absolute, complete well-being. I left having realized why so many people, since very ancient times, have worshiped the rising sun.

*

4. *Main Differences among the Great Religions*. Perhaps the most important difference between the religions originating in India and those originating in the Middle East is their concept of God and our relationship to It.

To the religions originating in India, God is everywhere, in all of nature, within us. Thus, God is absolutely close to us, most accessible, and easy to relate to. We can and should relate to It directly and individually, and establish a beautiful and rewarding relationship with It. We do not need mediators such as monks or priests between us and God. Most of the people who devote their lives to the practice and teaching of these Oriental religions, such as swamis or monks, are not mediators but instructors—just instructors of the activities they consider necessary for others to practice in order to get closer to God.

In the religions originating in the Middle East, especially Christianity, the concept prevails that God is above and beyond, far away from us, looking down from some distant point, observing everything we do in order to judge and punish. Thus, God is not easy to reach, not easy to relate to, too good to be near us. Here God is considered by most to be some powerful being mainly concerned with watching everything we do in order to approve or disapprove and, depending on our behavior, send us to heaven or to hell after death. We can relate to him individually, but we also definitely need the help of mediators who, supposedly, are much closer to God than any of us.

These two distinct ways of relating to God make a great difference to the millions of followers of the great religions. In the first there is the definite chance of establishing a real, positive, and beautiful relationship with God; but in the second, so many of these mediators, so far from God's truth and ways, often create confusion and negativity.

Another important difference is that the religions originating in India teach that we can experience the bliss of heaven here and now, that we can get to be "one with God" during this life on earth. It only depends on how close we get to God's harmony and will by conscious, daily practice of the right activities.

The religions originating in the Middle East, especially Christianity, mostly teach that, depending on our behavior here on earth and on God's judgment, we either become worthy, or not, of experiencing heaven, but only after we die, in the afterlife. We must wait till after death in order to get the best reward. Yet Judaism does not talk much about the afterlife.

The first concept is certainly more attractive, more compassionate, more Godlike. If we can attain the experience of heaven during this life on earth, then we have much more motivation to try to get closer to God's will, for it is *now* that we can be sure we are living and feeling. This concept seems more realistic and humane and makes life much more interesting.

The second point of view seems abstract, unrealistic, and unfair, imposing hard conditions for the highest prize and portraying God as a ruthless judge. It is a concept somehow devoid of God's compassion, constant help, and love, a concept which our hearts cannot really accept and which creates confusion in our minds.

The third significant difference is that the religions coming from India have no concept of sin. A man simply commits errors or mistakes and suffers the negative consequences, then learns from the negative experience not to commit the same negative actions again.

It is human to err and learn. It is a continuous learning process without guilty feelings, and this is why we are here. It is a process of getting ever closer to God's harmony by gradually learning to avoid negative actions. The spiritual pain and negative results of the experience will lead us to learn right from wrong.

The Middle Eastern dogmas, especially Christianity, mainly teach that we all are born sinners, that a man commits sins and that these negative actions can only be forgiven through repentance before God or through one of Its earthly representatives, a priest. Here a man is considered a sinner and deserves punishment and scorn.

This concept creates guilty feelings in individuals and the whole group who are constantly criticizing and judging one another, ready to start committing new sins since they can always be pardoned. Here it is difficult to learn and evolve for the better because improvement does not depend on us but on the will of God.

It becomes almost impossible to have healthy communities with the concept of men being eternal sinners, bad persons. This negative concept of sin certainly contributes to much of the aggression that constantly disturbs the relationships among human beings.

The teachings of the Great Masters have always been very clear and simple. It has been some of the disciples and organizers of religion who have established complicated and mysterious dogmas in order to appear as the only ones who understand God and who therefore act as mediators. As they appear to have spiritual ascendancy over the rest of the population, they can also exercise a great deal of control.

*

The night before, Candy and I had gone to a popular poetry reading and recited from memory "The Raven," that mind-blowing masterpiece by Edgar Allan Poe. She did one stanza; I did another, and so on until the end. It was a success; we had it well organized, memorized, and rehearsed.

I regret that most people who get acquainted with this extraordinary work of art do so in high school, most often through mediocre teachers, at an age when very few have the maturity to appreciate it—thus missing, usually forever, one of the greatest treasures the human spirit has ever offered.

If poetry were given more importance in our society, as it was at the peak of the splendid Greek civilization when poetry contests were held all over and prizes offered, I am sure it would be a better world. Poetry is such a great source of learning, transcending, understanding.

In spite of so many scientific and technological achievements, the general feeling of the world is dark and low because we are giving more importance to the lower material values of life than to the far more brilliant and higher values of the spirit.

It was such a thrill to successfully recite "The Raven" for all those people. To know the stillness and absolute silence that pervaded the audience during the performance. To finally hear the words of an elderly lady: "I have heard and read 'The Raven' many times, but never realized it was such a great poem."

*

5. *Religion, Politics, and Social Well-Being.* The main purpose of a religion is to help people understand themselves and improve their lives and their relationship with the rest of creation. It seems today that most are not succeeding; mankind is ever more out of harmony. Many people are more or less out of harmony with themselves and, therefore, with others and the environment.

Humanity is suffering from ever growing crime, deprivation, hunger, and misery. All over the world there are increasing millions of abandoned children falling in to crime, destitution, prostitution.

Is this Godlike, harmonious, right? Is not the world population increasing alarmingly out of balance and destroying themselves and the environment? Why is the supposedly superior human race, with all its scientific and technical achievements, creating such an expanding state of chaos? Is humanity really in control? Why so much destruction and misery, and who has the greatest share of responsibility?

The main cause of this worldly chaos is that many people all over are giving much more importance to material things than to those of the spirit, due to their own ignorance and confusion, much coming from the negative influences of most television programs.

Religious and political leaders have, no doubt, the greatest share of responsibility for whatever happens in the world, especially the leaders of the great religions since they have so much influence over the behavior of so many of the individuals that form humanity.

If some religious leaders had a higher level of consciousness, they would have recommended long ago that their followers only procreate the children that can be raised properly. When Jesus said "grow and multiply," he said it to a small number of people that lived under very different circumstances from our own; he meant "to grow and multiply as sons of God" while spreading the Truth. These religious leaders would strongly oppose the production of so many negative TV programs

At present, many of us are so far away from God's will and create such chaos on our planet, that, more than ever, it seems extremely urgent that we come closer to the natural laws of God in order to prevent total chaos and misery. It is obvious that we are not in control of what is happening in today's world. Ever increasing destruction, chaos, and misery is taking place at an alarming and tragic pace.

When we do not have higher levels of consciousness, it is easier to criticize new leaders or groups of people that are striving to regain the natural, spiritual values of humanity by different methods than our own, and be blind to the fact that it is mainly ignorance of reality and truth and, as a consequence, the intense cult for the material that is causing the tragic deterioration of life in the world.

Political leaders also have a great amount of responsibility for what is happening today. The political structure under which a particular population lives determines, to a great extent, their possibilities of reaching higher levels of education and evolution. Only the right kind of atmosphere enables us to better understand ourselves, positively evolve, and learn to live in harmony with our environment. When people do not have peace of mind, they can hardly create order and harmony around them.

It should be obvious to all important political leaders in today's world that decentralized democracies—where the states or provinces that form part of a country have a high degree of political and economic freedom, where there is a multiparty system that allows people to elect freely and directly the functionaries that will represent them at every level of government, and where power is balanced among the three branches of government, which effectively control each other—are the only political structures that really promote social well-being and economic prosperity, the political structures that really favor human evolution.

It should also be obvious that centralized or totalitarian political structures create a negative atmosphere under which human beings do not feel good and, as a result, do not work well. If there is no political freedom, there is no dignity, and without it there cannot be real social well-being to create economic prosperity. The human spirit chokes and rebels. Thus, no one can feel good, work well or take good care of natural responsibilities to community or country under politically negative circumstances.

All these facts are certainly clear to a really well-educated person, but there are not many really well-educated persons in the world. The general system of education in most countries is not good enough. The basic facts of life are not taught well, the concepts and facts about religion and politics, which are so crucial to the well-being of humanity, are not clear enough to the majority.

There are still many ignorant and mediocre political leaders all over the world, creating misery and negativity by maintaining centralized political regimes. And many others who, instead of doing what is right for their countries, are just playing politics or involved in corruption.

It is evident that the countries doing well and evolving better are those whose population enjoy the political freedom and dignity that only decentralized political structures can promote.

Mankind is at a crucial moment in its evolution; drastic changes have to be made in our way of approaching life if we want to successfully subsist and reach higher levels of evolution and well-being. Our numbers cannot keep growing at the rate they have been up to now; our production of material goods cannot continue to grow indefinitely and increasingly destroy the Earth. Drastic changes have to be made and many will suffer, but better to start now than later when the loss and suffering will be greater.

*

Riding the bicycle to the park was always enjoyable. But that day it was especially so. Spring had arrived, and the unusual quantity of flowers caught my attention and filled me with pleasure.

I had to go slowly and look at all those flowers as I rode along the many private gardens on the way.

Fortunately, most of the gardens had no fences, and it was possible to see the colorful, enchanting variety of well-kept trees, plants, and flowers.

I especially enjoyed looking at some very tall trees, usually found near the road, quite full of bright red flowers which almost covered the road underneath when they fell.

I decided to visit the botanical gardens nearby. It was the right time.

*

6. *Basic Measures to Improve Living Conditions in the World.*

A. *Decentralized Democracies*. As already mentioned, a decentralized political structure is the only political system that creates the circumstances where dignity and fairness can prevail, thus making people feel good, motivated to work and improve their lives in every sense. Therefore, the more advanced nations should do all they respectfully can to help promote and maintain decentralized democracies all over the world. The lack of decentralized political structures is the main reason that so many countries are still underdeveloped.

All human beings are basically the same. We all have the same basic needs: food, shelter, work, love. We do not need to be literate to know good from bad. We all have accurate feelings. When we live under an unfair political system, we know it and we resent it; when we live under a fair political system, we feel good and respond positively to it. So the only way to evolve for the better is to be exposed to a fair and open system that motivates us to take advantage of the opportunity to do what feels right, and by our actions discover our own potential, and so on. For some people it takes longer to learn, but at least there is hope. With a totalitarian system there is little hope; it is very difficult to evolve for the better. A negative atmosphere pervades all.

Decentralized democracies result from the natural evolution of human nature. Totalitarian regimes result from the minds of individuals with lower levels of consciousness and go against human nature. Totalitarian systems are doomed to disappear as awareness and education increase in a world of advanced communications systems.

B. *Instruction on Spiritual Religious Evolution.* It is absurd and surprising that the process of spiritual-religious development of mankind, which is the most important manifestation of human evolution, is practically ignored in most schools of the world.

As many of us know, since the very beginning of man's evolution towards higher levels of civilization, some kind of spiritual worship is to be found. Spiritual and religious activities have played an important role in the daily lives of most human beings since time immemorial. Spiritual inspiration or religious motivation has caused many of the most important actions in human history, and has driven, with incredible energy, many individuals or communities to perform glorious actions or extremely negative ones.

Thus, it is obvious that human beings have a very strong and interesting spiritual-religious history. To ignore this is to be out of touch with reality.

Why then are such important subjects as "History of Mankind's Spiritual Evolution" or "History of Religions" not taught in most schools?

We all must learn about these subjects. We all should grow up knowing something about prehistoric worship, tribal cults, ancient and modern religions. We all should know something about the many different ways we have worshipped since we started to do it. We all should be much more aware of our spiritual potential in order to understand ourselves better, learn to live better, and create better communities and better countries.

When are we finally going to learn what millenniums of history have constantly and clearly shown? That all great civilizations have resulted from a powerful spiritual drive, only to later decay and fall because they became too materialistic.

It is certainly amazing to realize how difficult it is for us to learn the simple fact that we must take care of our spiritual needs in order to really experience and enjoy life.

Yes, if we definitely want to improve living conditions in the world and truly evolve towards higher levels of civilization, the religious-spiritual evolution of mankind should be taught in schools all over. We all should know from the start that we have a wonderful, powerful, noble, and creative spiritual potential which is precisely what makes us human beings.

C. *Prayer in School.* It would certainly improve the world situation in the short and the long run, if children and teenagers all over would start their day by communicating with their Creator, by establishing a positive relationship with that High Spiritual Force that is within them and everywhere. They should be helped to know that there is a higher meaning and a higher purpose to their daily actions. They should feel positively motivated to cope with whatever daily task or circumstance they encounter.

We all should start our day with the consciousness that whatever we do or learn is for the higher purpose of evolving towards becoming better human beings, towards creating better communities and a better world, towards really enjoying life. We should start our day with the consciousness that whatever we do, we can do it in high spirits, feeling good, and enjoying it, that whatever we do, we can also help others feel good.

Thus, since very few households start their day with a positive uplifting prayer, this should certainly be a mandatory activity in all schools around the world—but not a prayer representative of any particular religion, for this would bring negativity and establish barriers. Just a simple, positive prayer directly expressed to our Creator, the one and only Universal Father.

Here is an example of such a prayer:

> Good morning, dear Creator, thank you for giving me the opportunity to experience a new day.
>
> Thank you for your constant guidance, your constant love, your protection, and all the good things I have.
>
> I want to dedicate this day to serving you and learning to improve myself, guided by the lessons I get from everything I do and everything that happens to me. Please help me follow your guidance so that I can achieve this goal.
>
> I must be careful with all my words and actions, for everything I say and do makes a difference.
>
> I should love and respect every person I relate to, for You are in all, and we are all equal.

Please, Father, help me to really be with you so that I can feel good, do good, and enjoy life.

Thank you, Father, thank you.

D. *Contests and Prizes for Outstanding Creativity and Achievements.* If contests were held and prizes awarded to the best manifestations of creativity and outstanding achievements in different levels of communities such as schools, towns, county seats, state capitals, and national capitals, life in the world would evolve much better—more balanced, enjoyable, and interesting. It would be like launching humanity toward higher levels of civilization and contentment and driving it away from negative escapism and low level, degrading entertainment. Drug consumption would be drastically reduced since it is basically the result of confusion, ignorance, idleness, and spiritual emptiness. It makes more sense to spend millions promoting naturally high spiritual experiences than to spend billions fighting drug distribution. Instead of spending money on negative drugs, people would be paid, through contests and prizes, to naturally experience higher and steadier feelings than the ones offered by drugs. Younger, deprived populations would have a better chance of becoming healthy, positive citizens.

*

During those days, I was reading extensively about the life of Alexander the Great. I very rarely read fiction, but a friend whom I trust, recommended very specially two historical novels about the life of the Macedonian king.

Like many other people, I knew that this was an extraordinary man who had created an enormous empire before he turned thirty years old. Yet, I knew very little about his ideas, his way of life, or the known details of his many campaigns and battles. He was all the more interesting because he lived at the peak of the marvelous Greek civilization, in a world supposedly very different from ours, with different concepts about some of the most important facts of life.

These two fascinating novels by Mary Renault—which I mostly read aloud, little by little, at nights—based mainly on real facts of his life, introduced me to a fantastic human being, who lived one of the most exciting and extraordinary lives ever lived.

These two books left me so interested in knowing more about this exceptional man that I subsequently read *The Campaigns of Alexander,* a book by Arrian, a Greek general and writer who lived later on. Then, I also read the long chapter dedicated to him by Plutarch, the Greek historian, in his book about the lives of great men of his time.

I realized that I wanted to know more about this very special man in order to learn more about myself and others. In any case, knowing more about Alexander the Great has been an enormous source of energy and faith in the human spirit.

*

7. *Relationships with Other People and Material Things.* As we reach higher levels of consciousness, we come to a point beyond any kind of bias or prejudice, and we become able to relate to life and all kinds of people with a wonderful and enjoyable freedom.

Any man can get to feel so good and high as to enter a dimension or level where he can relate on an equal basis to any other person, no matter how famous, rich, or well-educated that person may be.

When we prefer some people to others, this should depend on their degree of education or level of consciousness—simply because it is much nicer to relate to well-educated persons. Education is the only fact that, in a sense, makes one man different from another, the only fact that makes one man do better and behave better than another. Those who try to choose their friends for any other reason than genuine personal attraction or common interests are blind to truth, have a lower level of consciousness, and will never have real friends. Moreover, we do not choose real friends, they are given to us.

We must never feel less than anyone who has more material things than we have. For the best of life, to be sure, cannot be bought with money. A man who reaches higher levels of conscious-ness feels much better and is much happier than one who has great amounts of material goods but a lower level of consciousness.

No one can hide how one feels or how one approaches life. By the things we say or don't say or by the things we do or don't do, we are continually showing the level of consciousness we are on and how we approach life. To a man who has reached higher levels of consciousness and education, life becomes quite clear. He also knows the real source of well-being, and that material things are a lower and limited source of satisfaction.

Reaching high levels of consciousness and education usually requires a long and constant effort, a lot of energy and patience, many years of working on ourselves—usually a bigger effort than required to make large amounts of material things. It is very difficult to reach both in a lifetime.

Instead, feel sorry for those that mostly strive for material things; they are usually missing the highest and most exciting feelings, the best life has to offer. They will never be free from anguish or stress, for they do not take care of their spiritual needs. Be sure that everyone has a soul that subtly but strongly requires proper care, and the only way to really feel good is by regularly responding to that inner call.

Do not be fooled by material appearances; the more show, the less real satisfaction and happiness there is. Those who live expe-riencing the higher and best things in life, know better than to show off their material things. Only people with lower levels of consciousness and education show off their goods; not feeling really good about themselves, it is the easiest way to attract others. But whom do they attract? People similar to them, playing the same game, not capable of giving the best.

Thus, let us not be fooled and envy others. Let us just learn to support ourselves decently, and then let us work constantly to be our real selves and to ever feel good and high, then material goods will follow.

*

Yes, it was another beautiful day in south Miami, bright and clear and crisp.

I was looking forward to the evening. Adriana had invited me to see *Quest of Fire*, a film about prehistoric men and the meaningful moment when, after thousands of years of hard living on planet Earth, they discover how to make fire, a crucial step in their long evolution that would eventually lead them to discover a far more meaningful and burning fire—the fire within.

Make yourself an island,
Work hard, learn to be wise;
When your impurities are blown away
And you are free of guilt,
You will enter
The heavenly world of the elect.

Krishna, *Bhagavad Gita*

If you ever forget the Lord your God,
You shall surely perish,
Just like the nations
That the Lord made perish before you.

Moses, *Deuteronomy* 8

He who applies himself to the Law
Brightens up this world,
Like the moon
When free of clouds.

Buddha, *Doctrine of the Buddha*

Let the gate of immortal salvation
Be open to all.
He who has ears,
Let him hear the Word and believe.

Buddha, *Doctrine of the Buddha*

Therefore, oh disciples,
Be you lamps unto yourselves.
Rely on yourselves,
Do not rely on external help.

Buddha, *Doctrine of the Buddha*

God never made a heaven and a hell for man;
We are creators and we make our own.

Jesus, *Aquarian Gospel* 22

I am one come
To break away the wall
That separates the sons of men.
In Holy Breath
There is no Greek, nor Jew, nor Persian,
Nor slave, nor freed;
For all are one.

Jesus, *Aquarian Gospel* 81

This people honor me with their lips
But their heart is far away from me.

Jesus, *Mark* 7

In the beginning was the Word,
And the word was with God,
And the Word was God.

Jesus, *John* 1

Oh serene soul!
Return to your Lord,
Joyful and pleasing in His sight.
Yes, join His servants
And enter His paradise!

Mohammed, *Koran* 89

Conclusion

Yes, there is a knowledge above all others which, in a way, encompasses them all. When we regularly practice activities to keep in touch with our souls, we come in ever closer and direct contact with God's Creative Energy, source of everything. We get to "know It." This contact gradually leads us to realize, to know, where all things come from, how everything relates, what the meaning of life really is, and eventually brings us to a perfectly beautiful and harmonious relationship with all of creation.

This practice is certainly the best to develop our limitless potential and thus make of our lives an ever enjoyable and marvelous adventure. Yet, it will only work for those who approach it with humility, sincerity, and patience.

Remember Jesus' words: "Knock and you shall enter, Seek and you shall find."

*

Now, as a tribute to American creativity and genius, a poem related to the main subject of this work, by perhaps the greatest American poet that has ever lived:

My Soul

A noiseless patient spider,
I mark'd where, on a little promontory,
It stood isolated.
Mark'd how,
To explore the vacant, vast surrounding,
It launched forth, filament and filament and filament,
Out of itself;
Ever unreeling them,
Ever tirelessly speeding them.

And you, Oh My Soul,
Where you stand surrounded,
Surrounded in measureless oceans of space,
Ceaselessly musing, venturing, throwing;
Seeking the spheres to connect them;
Till the bridge you will need be formed,
Till the ductile anchor hold,
Till the gossamer thread you fling,
Catch somewhere,
Oh you, My Soul.

Walt Whitman, 1819 - 1892

About the Author

AURELIO ARREAZA was born to a long-established Venezuelan family, whose European ancestors had been in South America for six or seven generations. He was raised in a socially confused, "conservative" atmosphere, typical of underdeveloped countries, and had a negative religious influence. Early in life, however, he started looking for a "direct contact with God," which he deeply felt as the only thing that could help him understand the real purpose of life and give him the strength to pursue it.

In addition to scholastic training, Aurelio was continuously trying to learn, through all available means, everything he could concerning man's most important questions. This quest led him to learn extensively about the human body, the human mind, and the often unacknowledged human soul.

He studied many books, exchanged knowledge with like-minded people, attended several learning centers, experienced various theories and disciplines concerning human evolution, and finally found—to his infinite relief and as a reward to his long quest—that precious "direct contact with God."

By then Aurelio had already graduated from Law School in Venezuela, pursued some entrepreneurial activities, and had begun living a "traditional" materialistic way of life—to which he felt less and less attracted. Looking for a more spiritually conducive and positive environment in which to continue his life, he left Venezuela and came to stay in the United States. After several more years of spiritual practice, he found himself writing, in a clear, orderly, and simple way, what he considers the most important knowledge concerning mankind: a practical method to gradually improve the quality of life and tune in with the rhythm of Universal Harmony.

To be able to work on the book, he took a part-time job driving a taxi in New York City while living at Sivananda Yoga Center. After five years of working on the manuscript, completing a new version each year, in January 1988 Aurelio published a book he called *The Highest*, and sold hundreds of copies to his taxi-cab passengers. This led to many interesting conversations and feedback, and by mid-1989, after four more revisions, he finally felt the task finished and named the new manuscript, *The Highest Knowledge*.

Aurelio is currently living at Kripalu Center for Yoga and Health in Lenox, Massachusetts—a place he considers an exemplary center for integral evolution. There he does his best to be a positive part of the community and improve his life in every way.